Miss Rosie's SPICE of LIFE QUILTS

Designs by
Carrie L. Nelson

LEISURE ARTS, INC.
Little Rock, Arkansas

Editorial staff
editor-in-chief: Susan White Sullivan
quilt publications director: Cheryl Johnson
special projects director: Susan Frantz Wiles
senior prepress director: Mark Hawkins
art publications director: Rhonda Shelby
technical editor: Lisa Lancaster
technical writer: Frances Huddleston
editorial writer: Susan McManus Johnson
art category manager: Lora Puls
lead graphic artist: Amy Temple
graphic artists: Jacob Casleton,
    Frances Huddleston, Dana Vaughn,
    and Janie Wright
imaging technicians: Brian Hall,
    Stephanie Johnson, and Mark R. Potter
photography manager: Katherine Laughlin
contributing photographer: Ken West
contributing photostylist: Sondra Daniel
publishing systems administrator: Becky Riddle
publishing systems assistant: Clint Hanson

Business staff
vice president and chief operations officer:
    Tom Siebenmorgen
director of finance and administration:
    Laticia Mull Dittrich
vice president, sales and marketing:
    Pam Stebbins
national accounts director: Martha Adams
sales and services director: Margaret Reinold
information technology director: Hermine Linz
controller: Francis Caple
vice president, operations: Jim Dittrich
comptroller, operations: Rob Thieme
retail customer service manager: Stan Raynor
print production manager: Fred F. Pruss

Library of Congress Control Number 2010920101
ISBN-13: 978-1-60140-661-3
ISBN-10: 1-60140-661-4

10 9 8 7 6 5 4 3 2 1

table of *Contents*

designer
Carrie L. Nelson

A quilt that is simply gorgeous, looks complex yet is astonishingly simple to piece must be a quilt by Carrie Nelson! Carrie reigns supreme at achieving perfect color balance in her work while keeping the super-scrappy, serendipitous feel that quilters adore. "The more fabrics I can use in each quilt I make," says Carrie, "the happier I am."

While Carrie is the creative side of Miss Rosie's Quilt Company, her irrepressible golden retriever Rosie is the other half of the popular design team. Rosie's job is providing comic relief with her antics *(fabric scraps look best when scattered through the house)*. She's also adept at reminding Carrie that there's more to life than work *(gourmet dog biscuits and car rides—windows open, please)*.

That shared joie de vivre is easy to see in *Spice of Life Quilts*. The 13 dreamy designs (including one quilt in two color ways) offer something for every creative mood. Enhance your home with a lovely composition of favorite fabrics, or make a breathtaking gift for someone special. Original quilts like these add happiness to your hobby and lots more flavor to life!

Whirligig

Pieced by Judy Adams.
Quilted by Diane Tricka.

Finished Quilt Size:
80^1/$_2$" x 80^1/$_2$"
(204 cm x 204 cm)

Finished Block Size:
12" x 12" (30 cm x 30 cm)

"I love easy quilts, as long as they don't look easy," Carrie says. "What I like about Whirligig is that it looks complicated at first glance. I also like that the direction of the pinwheel is very easily changed by alternating the position of a single piece in each of the four parts of the block. How cool is that?" The quilt was pieced for Carrie by her friend Judy Adams. It was Judy's husband, Jack who came up with a name for the quilt, for which Carrie was grateful. She says, "Every name that Judy and I tried just wasn't right. If not for Jack's inspiration, the quilt would still be The As-Yet Still Un-named Quilt—which isn't very catchy, is it?"

Yardage Requirements

Yardage is based on 43"/44" (109 cm/112 cm) wide fabric. Fat quarters are approximately 21" x 18" (53 cm x 46 cm).

- 18 fat quarters of assorted light print fabrics
- 24 fat quarters of assorted dark print fabrics
- $7/8$ yd (80 cm) of fabric for binding
- $7^1/_2$ yds (6.9 m) of fabric for backing

You will also need:

- 89" x 89" (226 cm x 226 cm) piece of batting

Cutting Out the Pieces

Follow **Rotary Cutting**, page 105, to cut fabric. All measurements include $1/4$" seam allowances.

From *each* light print fat quarter:

- Cut 1 strip $6^1/_2$" x 21". From this strip,
  - Cut 6 **rectangles** $6^1/_2$" x $2^1/_2$". Cut a total of 100 rectangles.
  - Cut 4 **medium squares** $2^7/_8$" x $2^7/_8$". Cut a total of 72 medium squares.
- Cut 2 strips $5^1/_4$" x 21". From these strips,
  - Cut 5 **large squares** $5^1/_4$" x $5^1/_4$". Cut a total of 88 large squares.
  - Cut 4 **medium squares** $2^7/_8$" x $2^7/_8$". Cut a total of 28 medium squares. You will need 100 (25 sets of 4 matching) medium squares.

From *each* dark print fat quarter:

- Cut 2 strips $5^1/_4$" x 21". From these strips,
  - Cut 5 **large squares** $5^1/_4$" x $5^1/_4$". Cut a total of 113 large squares.
  - Cut 2 **small squares** $2^1/_2$" x $2^1/_2$". Cut a total of 36 small squares.
- Cut 2 **strips** $2^1/_2$" x 21". Cut a total of 48 strips.

Making the Flying Geese

Follow **Piecing**, page 106, and **Pressing**, page 107, to assemble the quilt top. Because there are so many seams in this quilt, you may need to use a seam allowance slightly smaller than the usual $1/4$". As you sew, measure your work to compare with the measurements provided and adjust your seam allowance as needed.

1. Draw a diagonal line (corner to corner) on wrong side of each light print **medium square**.
2. For 4 matching **Flying Geese**, select 4 matching light **medium squares** and 1 dark **large square**.
3. Matching right sides, place 1 **medium square** on opposite corners of **large square** (Fig. 1); pin in place.
4. Stitch $1/4$" from each side of drawn lines (Fig. 2). Cut along drawn lines to make 2 **Unit 1**'s. Press seam allowances to light fabrics.

Fig. 1

Fig. 2

Unit 1 (make 2)

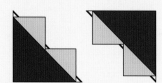

5. Matching corners, place 1 **medium square** on each **Unit 1** (Fig. 3).

6. Stitch seam $1/4$" from each side of drawn lines (Fig. 4). Cut along drawn lines to make 4 matching Flying Geese. Press seam allowances to light fabric. Flying Geese should measure $2^1/_2$" x $4^1/_2$" including seam allowances.

7. Repeat Steps 2–6 to make 25 sets of 4 matching Flying Geese.

Making the Hourglasses

1. Set aside 2 matching light **large squares** and 2 matching dark **large squares** for outer corners of quilt top. Draw a diagonal line (corner to corner) on wrong side of each remaining light **large square**.

2. Matching right sides, place 1 marked light **large square** on top of 1 dark **large square**. Stitch $1/4$" from each side of drawn line (Fig. 5). Cut along drawn line and press seam allowances to dark fabric to make 2 Triangle-Squares. Triangle-Square should measure $4^7/_8$" x $4^7/_8$" including seam allowances. Make 172 Triangle-Squares.

3. On wrong side of half of **Triangle-Squares**, draw a diagonal line (corner to corner and perpendicular to seam).

4. Matching right sides and seams and with light fabrics facing dark fabrics, place 1 marked **Triangle-Square** on top of 1 unmarked **Triangle-Square**. Stitch $1/4$" from each side of drawn line (Fig. 6). Cut apart along drawn line to make 2 Hourglasses; press seam allowances to one side. Hourglass should measure $4^1/_2$" x $4^1/_2$" including seam allowances. Make 172 Hourglasses.

Fig. 3

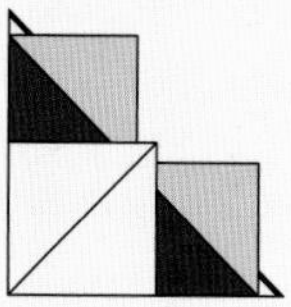

Fig. 4

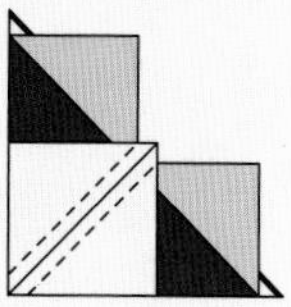

Flying Geese (make 25 sets of 4 matching)

Fig. 5

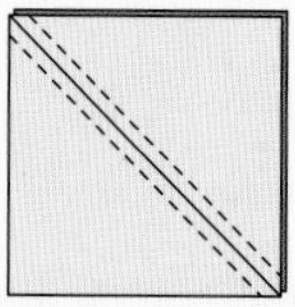

Triangle-Square (make 172)

Fig. 6

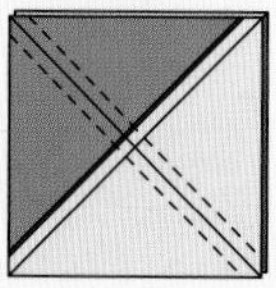

Hourglass (make 172)

Assembling the Blocks

Six of the Blocks in the quilt shown are "Alternate Blocks," which have the pinwheel turned the opposite direction. You may make as many of these Alternate Blocks as you wish. You will need a total of 25 Blocks.

1. For **Block**, select 4 matching **Flying Geese**, 4 assorted **Hourglasses**, and 4 assorted light **rectangles**.

2. Sew 1 **Flying Geese** and 1 **Hourglass** together to make **Unit 2**. Press seam allowances open or to Hourglass. Make 4 Unit 2's.

3. Sew 1 **Unit 2** and 1 **rectangle** together to make **Unit 3**. Press seam allowances to rectangle. Unit 3 should measure $6^1/_2$" x $6^1/_2$" including seam allowances. Make 4 Unit 3's.

4. Sew 4 **Unit 3's** together and press seam allowances open or as shown by arrows (**Fig. 7**) to make **Block**. Block should measure $12^1/_2$" x $12^1/_2$" including seam allowances.

5. For **Alternate Block**, repeat Steps 1–2. Sew **rectangle** to opposite side of **Unit 2** to make **Alternate Unit 3**. Make 4 Alternate Unit 3's.

6. Sew 4 **Alternate Unit 3's** together to make **Alternate Block**.

Making the Sashings

1. Sew 6 **strips** together to make **Strip Set**. Press seam allowances in one direction. Make 8 Strip Sets. Cut across Strip Sets at $2^1/_2$" intervals to make 60 **sashings**. Sashing should measure $2^1/_2$" x $12^1/_2$" including seam allowances.

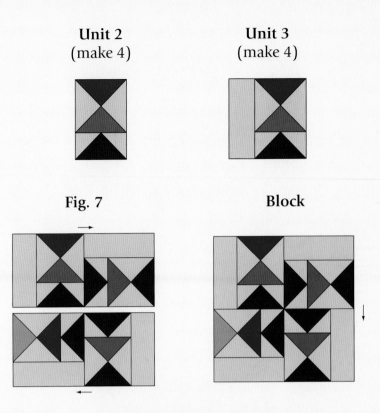

Unit 2
(make 4)

Unit 3
(make 4)

Fig. 7

Block

Alternate Unit 3 (make 4)

Alternate Block

Strip Set
(make 8)

Sashing
(make 60)

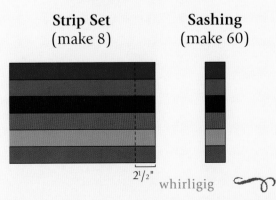

$2^1/_2$"

Assembling the Quilt Top Center

1. Sew 6 **small squares** and 5 **sashings** together to make Sashing Row. Press seam allowances to sashings. Sashing Row should measure $2^1/2$" x $72^1/2$" including seam allowances. Make 6 Sashing Rows.

2. Sew 6 **sashings** and 5 **Blocks** together to make **Block Row**. Press seam allowances to sashings. Block Row should measure $12^1/2$" x $72^1/2$" including seam allowances. Make 5 Block Rows.

3. Referring to **Quilt Top Diagram**, sew **Rows** together to make quilt top center. Press seam allowances to Sashing Rows. Quilt top center should measure $72^1/2$" x $72^1/2$" including seam allowances.

Adding the Border

1. For **border corners**, you will use the 2 light **large squares** and 2 dark **large squares** set aside earlier. Trim the 2 light large squares to $4^7/8$" x $4^7/8$".

2. Draw a diagonal line (corner to corner) on wrong side of each light **large square** and 1 dark **large square**.

3. Matching right sides, place marked dark **large square** on top of unmarked dark **large square**. Stitch $^1/4$" from each side of drawn line (**Fig. 8**). Cut along drawn line and press seam allowances to one side to make 2 **Triangle-Squares**. Triangle-Square should measure $4^7/8$" x $4^7/8$" including seam allowances

4. With right sides together and with drawn line on large square perpendicular to seam on Triangle-Square, place 1 light **large square** on top of 1 **Triangle-Square**. Stitch $^1/4$" from each side of drawn line (**Fig. 9**). Cut apart along drawn line to make 2 **border corners**; press seam allowances to one side. Border corner should measure $4^1/2$" x $4^1/2$" including seam allowances. Make 4 border corners.

5. Sew 18 **Hourglasses** together to make border. Press seam allowances open or in one direction. Make 4 borders.

6. Measure *length* across center of quilt top. Measure length of 2 borders for **side borders**. If measurements are not the same, make seams in borders slightly larger or smaller as needed. Do not sew side borders to quilt top center at this time.

Sashing Row (make 6)

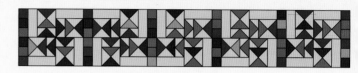

Block Row (make 5)

Fig. 8

Triangle-Square (make 2)

Fig. 9

Border Corner (make 4)

Border (make 4)

7. Measure *width* across center of quilt top. Measure length of 2 remaining borders for **top/bottom borders**. If measurements are not the same, make seams in borders slightly larger or smaller as needed. Sew 1 **border corner** to each end of top/bottom borders. Do not sew top/bottom borders to quilt top center at this time.

8. Matching centers and corners, sew **side**, **top**, and then **bottom borders** to quilt top center. Quilt top should measure $80\frac{1}{2}$" x $80\frac{1}{2}$" including seam allowances.

Completing the Quilt

1. To help stabilize the edges and prevent any seams from separating, stay-stitch around the quilt top approximately $\frac{1}{8}$" from the edge.
2. Follow **Quilting**, page 108, to mark, layer, and quilt as desired. Quilt shown was machine quilted. The dark triangles and outer seams of the Blocks were quilted in the ditch. A swirling feather pattern was quilted in each Block. An X was quilted in each square of the sashings. The inner seams and light triangles in the border were quilted in the ditch. Also in the border, a straight line design was quilted in the light areas and a looped design was quilted in the dark areas.
3. Follow **Making a Hanging Sleeve**, page 109, if a hanging sleeve is desired.
4. Cut a 28" square of binding fabric. Follow **Binding**, page 110, to bind quilt using 2"w bias binding with mitered corners.

Note: This quilt is easily made smaller or larger by subtracting or adding Blocks to the length or width. Subtracting or adding a single Row or Column of Blocks will change the measurement by 14". Border will need to be adjusted.

Quilt Top Diagram

Double Duty

Quilted by Diane Tricka.

Finished Quilt Size:
$77^3/8$" x $77^3/8$"
(197 cm x 197 cm)

Finished Block Size:
6" x 6" (15 cm x 15 cm)

You have to love a quilt that looks complex at first glance—but isn't! Carrie is a marvel at finding ways to compose intricate-looking quilts using really simple blocks. The easy Log Cabin and Flying Geese Blocks in this quilt look more elaborate because they're set on the diagonal. The Double Duty part of this quilt has to do with the fact that Carrie needed "demo" pieces for a class. She planned to demonstrate her favorite methods for piecing Log Cabins and Flying Geese. And since she had fabric for a quilt that she hadn't yet designed, she decided to use that fabric for her demo pieces—which became the start of this quilt, Double Duty!

Yardage Requirements

Yardage is based on 43"/44" (109 cm/112 cm) wide fabric. Fat quarters are approximately 21" x 18" (53 cm x 46 cm).

> 7 fat quarters of assorted light print fabrics for Flying Geese and Log Cabin centers
> 10 fat quarters of assorted light print fabrics for Log Cabin Blocks
> 20 fat quarters of assorted dark print fabrics
> 1 yd (91 cm) of gold print fabric for setting triangles
> $^7/_8$ yd (80 cm) of fabric for binding
> $7^1/_4$ yds (6.6 m) of fabric for backing

You will also need:

> 86" x 86" (218 cm x 218 cm) piece of batting

Cutting Out the Pieces

Follow **Rotary Cutting**, page 105, to cut fabric. All measurements include $^1/_4$" seam allowances.

From *each* light print fat quarter for Flying Geese and Log Cabin centers:
- Cut 3 strips $3^7/_8$" x 21". From these strips,
  - Cut 12 **medium squares** $3^7/_8$" x $3^7/_8$". Cut a total of 80 (20 sets of 4 matching) medium squares.
- Cut 2 strips $2^7/_8$" x 21". From these strips,
  - Cut 8 **small squares** $2^7/_8$" x $2^7/_8$". Cut a total of 52 small squares.

From *each* light print fat quarter for Log Cabin Blocks:
- Cut 11 strips $1^1/_2$" x 21". Cut a total of 104 strips. From each strip,
  - Cut 1 **rectangle #1** $1^1/_2$" x $2^1/_2$". Cut a total of 104 rectangle #1's.
  - Cut 1 **rectangle #2** $1^1/_2$" x $3^1/_2$". Cut a total of 104 rectangle #2's.
  - Cut 1 **rectangle #5** $1^1/_2$" x $4^1/_2$". Cut a total of 104 rectangle #5's.
  - Cut 1 **rectangle #6** $1^1/_2$" x $5^1/_2$". Cut a total of 104 rectangle #6's.

From *each* dark print fat quarter:
- Cut 1 strip $7^1/_4$" x 21". From this strip,
  - Cut 1 **large square** $7^1/_4$" x $7^1/_4$". Cut a total of 20 large squares.
  - Cut 3 **small squares** $2^7/_8$" x $2^7/_8$". Cut a total of 52 small squares.
- Cut 6 strips $1^1/_2$" x 21". Cut a total of 104 strips. From *each* strip,
  - Cut 1 **rectangle #3** $1^1/_2$" x $3^1/_2$". Cut a total of 104 rectangle #3's.
  - Cut 1 **rectangle #4** $1^1/_2$" x $4^1/_2$". Cut a total of 104 rectangle #4's.
  - Cut 1 **rectangle #7** $1^1/_2$" x $5^1/_2$". Cut a total of 104 rectangle #7's.
  - Cut 1 **rectangle #8** $1^1/_2$" x $6^1/_2$". Cut a total of 104 rectangle #8's.

From gold print fabric for setting triangles:
- Cut 3 strips $10^1/_4$" wide by the width of the fabric. From these strips,
  - Cut 9 squares $10^1/_4$" x $10^1/_4$".
    - Cut 2 of these squares *once* diagonally to make 4 **corner setting triangles**.
    - Cut 7 of these squares *twice* diagonally to make 28 **side setting triangles**.

Making the Flying Geese Blocks

Follow **Piecing**, page 106, and **Pressing**, page 107, to assemble the quilt top. Because there are so many seams in this quilt, you may need to use a seam allowance slightly smaller than the usual ¹/₄". As you sew, measure your work to compare with the measurements provided and adjust your seam allowance as needed.

1. Draw a diagonal line (corner to corner) on wrong side of each light print **medium square**.
2. For 4 matching **Flying Geese**, select 4 matching light **medium squares** and 1 dark **large square**.
3. Matching right sides, place 1 **medium square** on opposite corners of **large square** (**Fig. 1**); pin in place.
4. Stitch ¹/₄" from each side of drawn lines (**Fig. 2**). Cut along drawn lines to make 2 **Unit 1's**. Press seam allowances to light fabrics.

Fig. 1

Fig. 2

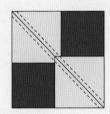

Unit 1 (make 2)

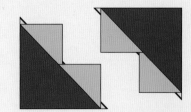

5. Matching corners, place 1 **medium square** on each **Unit 1** (**Fig. 3**).
6. Stitch seam $1/4$" from each side of drawn lines (**Fig. 4**). Cut along drawn lines to make 4 **Flying Geese**. Press seam allowances to light fabric. Flying Geese should measure $3^1/2$" x $6^1/2$" including seam allowances.
7. Repeat Steps 2–6 to make a total of 80 Flying Geese.
8. Sew 2 **Flying Geese** together to make **Flying Geese Block**. Press seam allowances open or to one side. Flying Geese Block should measure $6^1/2$" x $6^1/2$" including seam allowances. Make 40 Flying Geese Blocks.

Making the Log Cabin Blocks

1. Draw a diagonal line (corner to corner) on wrong side of each light **small square**.
2. Matching right sides, place 1 light **small square** on top of 1 dark **small square**. Stitch $1/4$" from each side of drawn line (**Fig. 5**). Cut along drawn line and press seam allowances to dark fabric to make 2 **Triangle-Squares**. Triangle-Square should measure $2^1/2$" x $2^1/2$" including seam allowances. Make a total of 104 Triangle-Squares.
3. Sew 1 **Triangle-Square** and 1 **rectangle #1** together to make **Unit 2**. Press seam allowances to rectangle #1.
4. Sew **Unit 2** and 1 **rectangle #2** together to make **Unit 3**. Press seam allowances to rectangle #2.
5. Sew **Unit 3** and 1 **rectangle #3** together to make **Unit 4**. Press seam allowances to rectangle #3.
6. Sew **Unit 4** and 1 **rectangle #4** together to make **Unit 5**. Press seam allowances to rectangle #4.
7. In the same manner, add **rectangles #5–#8** in numerical order to make **Log Cabin Block**, rotating Block and pressing each seam to last rectangle added. Block should measure $6^1/2$" x $6^1/2$" including seam allowances.
8. Repeat Steps 3–7 to make a total of 104 Log Cabin Blocks.

Fig. 3

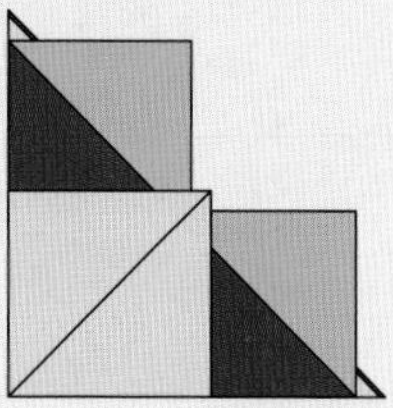

Fig. 4

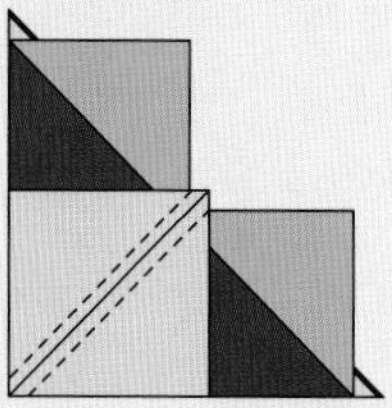

Flying Geese
(make 80)

Flying Geese Block
(make 40)

Fig. 5

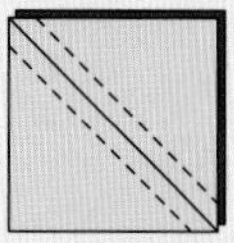

Triangle-Square
(make 104)

Unit 2

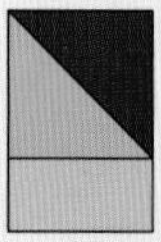

Unit 3

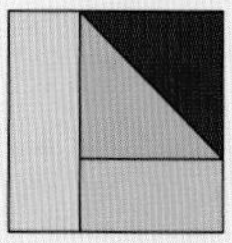

Unit 4

Unit 5

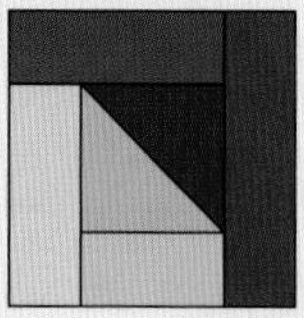

Log Cabin Block (make 104)

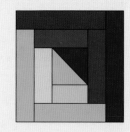

Assembling the Quilt Top

*Referring to **Assembly Diagram**, lay out Blocks and setting triangles into diagonal Rows. Pay attention to the positioning of the light and dark sides of the Log Cabin Blocks and to the direction of the Flying Geese. It's very easy to get them turned around, especially between the floor/design wall and the sewing machine.*
Note: *The setting triangles are slightly over-cut to allow the center pieced part of the quilt to "float."*

1. Sew **Blocks** and **side setting triangles** together into diagonal **Rows**. Press seam allowances open, or press in one direction on every other Row and the opposite direction in remaining Rows.

2. Sew **Rows** together, pressing seam allowances open or in one direction.

3. Sew **corner setting triangles** to quilt top. Press seam allowances open or to corner setting triangles. Trim corner setting triangles as needed to square quilt top. Quilt top should measure approximately $77^3/_8$" x $77^3/_8$" including seam allowances.

Completing the Quilt

1. To help stabilize the edges and prevent any seams from separating, stay-stitch around the quilt top approximately $^1/_8$" from the edge.

2. Follow **Quilting**, page 108, to mark, layer, and quilt as desired. Quilt shown was machine quilted. Leaf designs were quilted in the Flying Geese, Log Cabin Block centers, and setting triangles. Straight line designs were quilted in the Log Cabin Blocks.

3. Follow **Making a Hanging Sleeve**, page 109, if a hanging sleeve is desired.

4. Cut a 27" square of binding fabric. Follow **Binding**, page 110, to bind quilt using 2"w bias binding with mitered corners.

Assembly Diagram

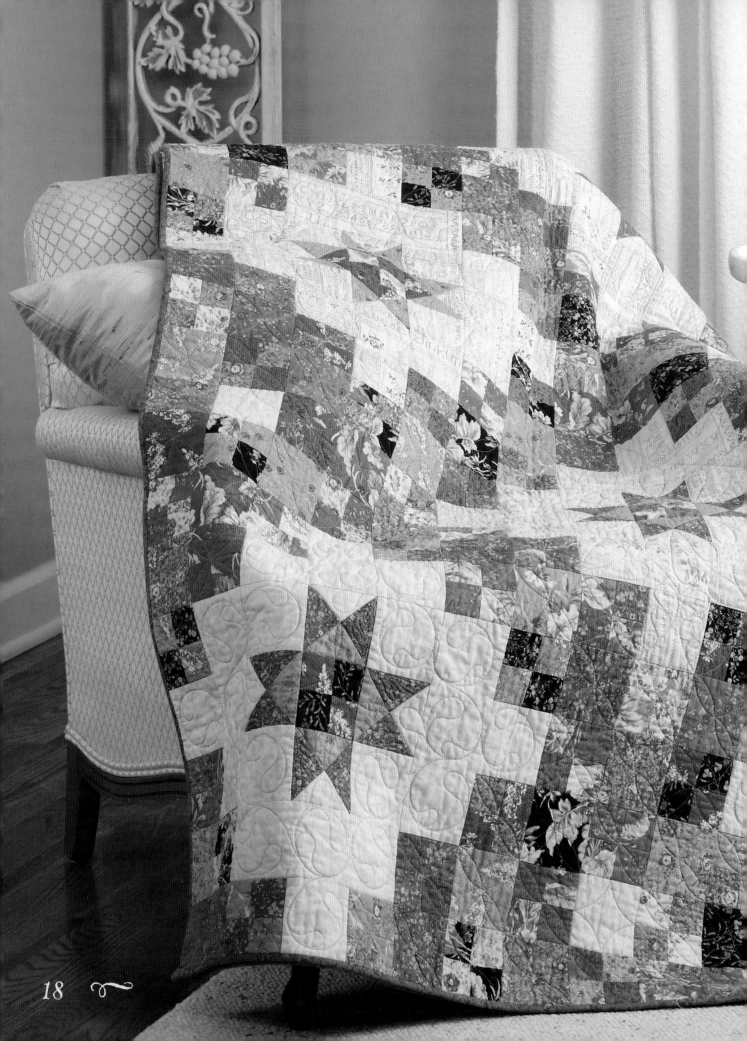

Ginger Belle

Quilted by Diane Tricka.

Finished Quilt Size:
81¹/₂" x 81¹/₂"
(207 cm x 207 cm)

Finished Block Size:
15" x 15" (38 cm x 38 cm)

As Carrie says, "Sometimes a quilt is just meant to be, because everything about it just fits." She was making some changes to the traditional Irish Chain design by making some of the Twenty-Five Patch squares into Four Patches when she decided to go a step further and add Ohio Stars to the open spaces between the "chains." "Hand-quilting the big white spaces or adding appliqués are wonderful options, but they just aren't me," Carrie says. "The Ohio Stars just happened to be a perfect fit! As for the quilt's name, the fabric line was named Rhubarb & Ginger. Also, since Ginger is the name of one of my favorite people (nicknamed Ginger Belle—it's a Steel Magnolias reference), it's a nice reminder of a wonderful person and friend."

19

Yardage Requirements

Yardage is based on 43"/44" (109 cm/112 cm) wide fabric. Fat quarters are approximately 21" x 18" (53 cm x 46 cm).

 13 fat quarters of assorted light print fabrics

 25 fat quarters of assorted dark print fabrics

 $^7/_8$ yd (80 cm) of fabric for binding

 $7^1/_2$ yds (6.9 m) of fabric for backing

You will also need:

 90" x 90" (229 cm x 229 cm) piece of batting

Cutting Out the Pieces

*Follow **Rotary Cutting**, page 105, to cut fabric. All measurements include $^1/_4$" seam allowances.*

From *each* light print fat quarter:

- Cut 1 strip $4^1/_4$" x 21". From this strip,
  - Cut 1 **large square** $4^1/_4$" x $4^1/_4$". Cut a total of 13 large squares.
  - Cut 4 **small squares** $3^1/_2$" x $3^1/_2$". Cut a total of 52 small squares.
- Cut 1 strip $3^1/_2$" x 21". From this strip,
  - Cut 5 **small squares** $3^1/_2$" x $3^1/_2$". Cut a total of 60 small squares. You will have 112 (13 sets of 8 matching and 8 assorted) small squares.
- Cut 2 strips $3^1/_2$" x 21". From these strips,
  - Cut 4 **rectangles** $3^1/_2$" x $9^1/_2$". Cut a total of 52 (13 sets of 4 matching) rectangles.

From *each* dark print fat quarter:

- Cut 1 strip $4^1/_4$" x 21". From this strip,
  - Cut 2 **large squares** $4^1/_4$" x $4^1/_4$". Cut a total of 39 (13 sets of 2 matching and 13 assorted) large squares.
- Cut 1 strip $3^1/_2$" x 21". From this strip,
  - Cut 6 **small squares** $3^1/_2$" x $3^1/_2$". Cut a total of 148 small squares.
- Cut 5 **strips** 2" x 21". Cut a total of 106 strips.

Making the Hourglasses

*Follow **Piecing**, page 106, and **Pressing**, page 107, to assemble the quilt top. Because there are so many seams in this quilt, you may need to use a seam allowance slightly smaller than the usual $^1/_4$". As you sew, measure your work to compare with the measurements provided and adjust your seam allowance as needed.*

1. For 4 matching **Hourglasses**, select 2 dark print **large squares** from 1 print (for star points), 1 dark print **large square** from a different print, and 1 light print **large square** (for background).

2. Draw a diagonal line (corner to corner) on wrong side of the 2 matching dark **large squares**.

3. Matching right sides, place 1 marked dark **large square** on top of unmarked dark **large square**. Stitch $^1/_4$" from each side of drawn line (**Fig. 1**). Cut along drawn line and press seam allowances to marked fabric to make 2 **Triangle-Square A's**. Triangle-Square A should measure $3^7/_8$" x $3^7/_8$" including seam allowances.

4. Use remaining marked **large square** and light print **large square** to make 2 **Triangle-Square B's**. Press seam allowances to marked fabric. Triangle-Square B should measure $3^7/_8$" x $3^7/_8$" including seam allowances.

Fig. 1

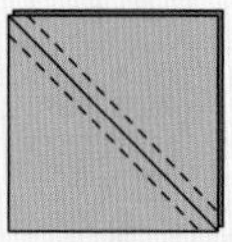

Triangle-Square A (make 2)

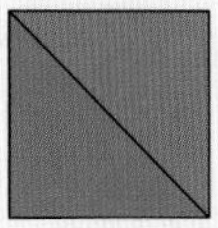

Triangle-Square B (make 2)

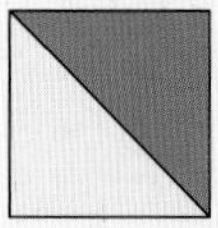

5. On wrong side of each **Triangle-Square B**, draw a diagonal line (corner to corner and perpendicular to seam).

6. Matching right sides and seams, place 1 **Triangle-Square B** on top of 1 **Triangle-Square A** with matching triangles opposite each other. Stitch ¹/₄" from each side of drawn line (**Fig. 2**). Cut apart along drawn line to make 2 **Hourglasses**. Press seam allowances to one side. Hourglass should measure 3¹/₂" x 3¹/₂" including seam allowances. Make 4 matching Hourglasses.

7. Repeat Steps 1–6 to make 13 sets of 4 matching Hourglasses.

Making the Four Patches

1. Sew 2 **strips** together to make **Strip Set**. Press seam allowances to one side. Make 53 Strip Sets. Cut across Strip Sets at 2" intervals to make 522 **Unit 1's**. Unit 1 should measure 2" x 3¹/₂" including seam allowances.

2. Sew 2 matching **Unit 1's** together to make **Four Patch**. To press seam allowances, follow **Collapsing the Seams**, page 107. Four Patch should measure 3¹/₂" x 3¹/₂" including seam allowances. Make 261 Four Patches.

Making the Ohio Star Blocks

1. For **Ohio Star Block**, select 4 matching **Hourglasses**, 4 light **small squares** and 4 light **rectangles** of the same fabric as the light triangle in these Hourglasses, and 5 assorted **Four Patches**.

2. Sew 2 light **small squares** and 1 **Hourglass** together to make **Unit 2**. Press seam allowances to small squares. Make 2 Unit 2's.

3. Sew 2 **Hourglasses** and 1 **Four Patch** together to make **Unit 3**. Press seam allowances to Four Patch.

4. Sew 2 **Unit 2's** and **Unit 3** together to make **Unit 4**. Press seam allowances to Unit 3. Unit 4 should measure 9¹/₂" x 9¹/₂" including seam allowances.

5. Sew 2 **Four Patches** and 1 **rectangle** together to make **Unit 5**. Press seam allowances to rectangle. Make 2 **Unit 5's**.

6. Sew 2 **rectangles** and **Unit 4** together to make **Unit 6**. Press seam allowances to rectangles.

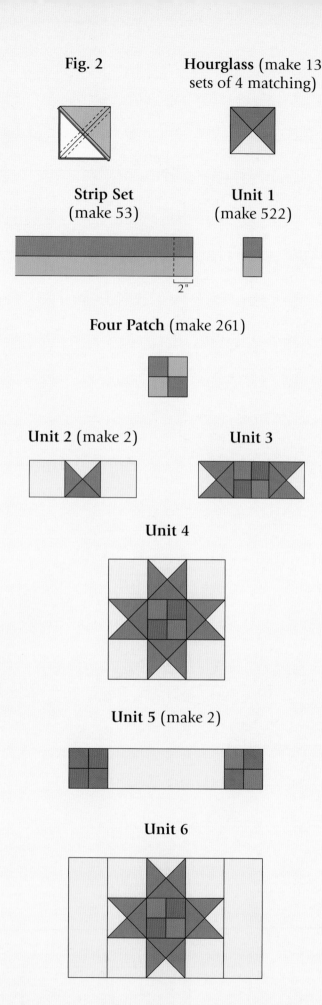

Fig. 2

Hourglass (make 13 sets of 4 matching)

Strip Set (make 53)

Unit 1 (make 522)

2"

Four Patch (make 261)

Unit 2 (make 2)   **Unit 3**

Unit 4

Unit 5 (make 2)

Unit 6

7. Sew 2 **Unit 5's** and **Unit 6** together to make Ohio Star Block. Press seam allowances to Unit 6. Ohio Star Block should measure $15^1/_2$" x $15^1/_2$" including seam allowances.

8. Repeat Steps 1–7 to make a total of 13 Ohio Star Blocks.

Making the Irish Chain Blocks

Refer to Quilt Top Diagram, page 25, to arrange your Ohio Star Blocks on a floor or design wall. Arrange pieces for each Irish Chain Block beside or between the Ohio Star Blocks, placing the same light fabric in the area around each star.

1. For **Irish Chain Block**, select 4 light print **small squares**, 9 assorted dark print **small squares**, and 12 assorted **Four Patches**.

2. Sew 2 dark print **small squares**, 1 light print **small square**, and 2 **Four Patches** together to make Unit 7. Press seam allowances to small squares. Make 2 Unit 7's.

3. Sew 3 **Four Patches** and 2 dark print **small squares** together to make Unit 8. Press seam allowances to small squares. Make 2 Unit 8's.

4. Sew 2 light print **small squares**, 1 dark print **small square**, and 2 **Four Patches** together to make Unit 9. Press seam allowances to small squares.

5. Sew 2 **Unit 7's**, 2 **Unit 8's**, and **Unit 9** together to make Irish Chain Block. Press seam allowances away from Unit 8's. Irish Chain Block should measure $15^1/_2$" x $15^1/_2$" including seam allowances.

6. Repeat Steps 1–5 to make 12 Irish Chain Blocks.

Ohio Star Block (make 13)

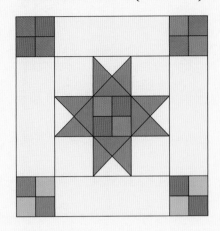

Unit 7 (make 2)

Unit 8 (make 2)

Unit 9

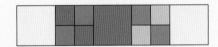

Irish Chain Block (make 12)

Assembling the Quilt Top Center

Remember to pay attention to the placement of the light print small squares.

1. Sew 3 **Ohio Star Blocks** and 2 **Irish Chain Blocks** together to make **Row A**. Press seam allowances open or to Irish Chain Blocks. Row A should measure 15$^1/_2$" x 75$^1/_2$" including seam allowances. Make 3 Row A's.

2. Sew 3 **Irish Chain Blocks** and 2 **Ohio Star Blocks** together to make **Row B**. Press seam allowances open or to Irish Chain Blocks. Row B should measure 15$^1/_2$" x 75$^1/_2$" including seam allowances. Make 2 Row B's.

3. Sew **Rows** together to make quilt top center. Press seam allowances open or in one direction. Quilt top center should measure 75$^1/_2$" x 75$^1/_2$" including seam allowances.

Adding the Borders

Continue to pay attention to the placement of the light print small squares.

1. Sew 12 **Four Patches**, 10 dark **small squares**, and 3 light **small squares** together to make **side border**. Press seam allowances to small squares. Make 2 side borders.

2. To add **side borders**, measure *length* across center of quilt top. Measure length of side borders. If measurements are not the same, make seams in borders slightly larger or smaller as needed. Matching centers and corners, sew side borders to quilt top center.

3. Sew 14 **Four Patches**, 10 dark **small squares**, and 3 light **small squares** together to make **top border**. Press seam allowances to small squares. Repeat to make **bottom border**.

4. To add **top/bottom borders**, measure *width* across center of quilt top (including added borders). Measure length of top/bottom borders. If measurements are not the same, make seams in borders slightly larger or smaller as needed. Matching centers and corners, sew top/bottom borders to quilt top center. Quilt top should measure 81$^1/_2$" x 81$^1/_2$" including seam allowances.

Row A (make 3)

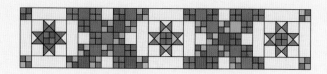

Row B (make 2)

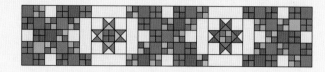

Side Border (make 2)

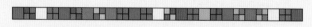

Top/Bottom Border (make 2)

Completing the Quilt

1. To help stabilize the edges and prevent any seams from separating, stay-stitch around the quilt top approximately $^1/_8$" from the edge.

2. Follow **Quilting**, page 108, to mark, layer, and quilt as desired. Quilt shown was machine quilted. Swirling motifs were quilted around each star and four leaves were quilted in each Four Patch and dark small square. Meandering quilting was quilted in the points of the stars.

3. Follow **Making a Hanging Sleeve**, page 109, if a hanging sleeve is desired.

4. Cut a 28" square of binding fabric. Follow **Binding**, page 110, to bind quilt using 2"w bias binding with mitered corners.

Three Coins

Quilted by LeAnne Olson.

Finished Quilt Size:
72¹/₂" x 72¹/₂"
(184 cm x 184 cm)

Finished Block Size:
12" x 12" (30 cm x 30 cm)

Do you ever dream about quilts? That's how Carrie came up with this quilt. She had another layout in mind while she made the red Star Blocks, but once they were done, she knew the setting she'd planned wasn't right. So she put the red stars aside and worked on something else for a while. Then one day, she woke up with the perfect setting in mind. "I love it, as it is exactly what I wanted my quilt to look like. But here's my question—I dreamed of something wonderful, and it happened. So, why hasn't George Clooney shown up on my doorstep yet?" Three Coins got its name from one of Carrie's favorite old movies, Three Coins in a Fountain.

Yardage Requirements

Yardage is based on 43"/44" (109 cm/112 cm) wide fabric. Fat quarters are approximately 21" x 18" (53 cm x 46 cm).

> 8 fat quarters of assorted cream print fabrics for Star Blocks
> 7 fat quarters of assorted light print fabrics for large Triangle-Squares
> 4 fat quarters of assorted red print fabrics
> 4 fat quarters of assorted green print fabrics
> 4 fat quarters of assorted gold print fabrics
> 4 fat quarters of assorted blue print fabrics
> $7/8$ yd (80 cm) of fabric for binding
> $6^3/4$ yds (6.2 m)* of fabric for backing

You will also need:

> 81" x 81" (206 cm x 206 cm) piece of batting

*Yardage is based on 3 lengths of fabric, which allows for a larger backing for long arm quilting. If you are using another quilting method, 2 lengths or $4^1/2$ yds (4.1 m) will be adequate.

Cutting Out the Pieces

*Follow **Rotary Cutting**, page 105, to cut fabric. All measurements include $1/4$" seam allowances.*

From *each* cream print fat quarter:

- Cut 1 strip $5^1/4$" x 21". From this strip,
  - Cut 2 **large squares** $5^1/4$" x $5^1/4$". Cut a total of 16 large squares.
    From remainder of strip,
    - Cut 2 strips $2^1/2$" x $10^1/2$". From these strips,
      - Cut 8 **very small squares** $2^1/2$" x $2^1/2$". Cut a total of 64 (16 sets of 4 matching) very small squares.
- Cut 2 strips $2^7/8$" x 21". From these strips,
  - Cut 12 **small squares** $2^7/8$" x $2^7/8$". Cut a total of 96 (16 sets of 6 matching) small squares.
- Cut 2 strips $2^1/2$" x 21". From these strips,
  - Cut 8 **rectangles** $2^1/2$" x $4^1/2$". Cut a total of 64 (16 sets of 4 matching) rectangles.

From *each* light print fat quarter:

- Cut 2 strips $6^7/8$" x 21". From these strips,
  - Cut 6 **very large squares** $6^7/8$" x $6^7/8$". Cut a total of 40 very large squares.

From *each* red print fat quarter:

- Cut 2 strips $5^1/4$" x 21". From these strips,
  - Cut 4 **large squares** $5^1/4$" x $5^1/4$". Cut a total of 16 large squares.
- Cut 2 strips $2^7/8$" x 21". From these strips,
  - Cut 8 **small squares** $2^7/8$" x $2^7/8$". Cut a total of 32 (16 sets of 2 matching) small squares.

From *each* green print fat quarter:

- Cut 1 strip $3^5/16$" x 21". From this strip,
  - Cut 4 **medium squares** $3^5/16$" x $3^5/16$". (**Note:** $3^5/16$" is halfway between the $3^1/4$" and $3^3/8$" marks on your ruler.) Cut a total of 16 medium squares.
- Cut 3 strips $2^7/8$" x 21". From these strips,
  - Cut 16 **small squares** $2^7/8$" x $2^7/8$". Cut a total of 64 (16 sets of 4 matching) small squares.

From *each* of 3 gold print fat quarters:

- Cut 2 strips $6^7/8$" x 21". From these strips,
  - Cut 6 **very large squares** $6^7/8$" x $6^7/8$". Cut a total of 18 very large squares.

From remaining gold print fat quarter:

- Cut 5 strips $2^7/8$" x 21". From these strips,
  - Cut 32 squares $2^7/8$" x $2^7/8$". Cut squares once diagonally to make 64 (16 sets of 4 matching) **triangles**.

From *each* blue print fat quarter:

- Cut 2 strips $6^7/8$" x 21". From these strips,
  - Cut 6 **very large squares** $6^7/8$" x $6^7/8$". Cut a total of 22 very large squares.

Making the Star Blocks

Follow **Piecing**, page 106, and **Pressing**, page 107, to assemble the quilt top. Because there are so many seams in this quilt, you may need to use a seam allowance slightly smaller than the usual $^1/_4$". As you sew, measure your work to compare with the measurements provided and adjust your seam allowance as needed.

1. For **Star Block**, select 1 **large square**, 6 **small squares**, 4 **very small squares**, and 4 **rectangles** from 1 cream print fabric. Select 1 **medium square** and 4 **small squares** from 1 green print fabric. Select 1 **large square** and 2 **small squares** from 1 red print. You will also need 4 matching gold **triangles**.

2. Draw a diagonal line (corner to corner) on wrong side of each green **small square** and each cream **small square**.

3. For 4 matching **Flying Geese A's**, use 4 green **small squares** and cream **large square**.

4. Matching right sides, place 1 **small square** on opposite corners of **large square** (Fig. 1); pin in place.

5. Stitch ¹/₄" from each side of drawn lines (Fig. 2). Cut along drawn lines to make 2 **Unit 1's**. Press seam allowances to green fabric.

6. Matching corners, place 1 **small square** on each **Unit 1** (Fig. 3).

7. Stitch seam ¹/₄" from each side of drawn lines (Fig. 4). Cut along drawn lines to make 4 **Flying Geese A's**. Press seam allowances to green fabric. Flying Geese A should measure 2¹/₂" x 4¹/₂" including seam allowances.

8. Using 4 cream **small squares** and red **large square**, repeat Steps 4–7 to make 4 **Flying Geese B's**. Press seam allowances to cream fabric. Flying Geese B should measure 2¹/₂" x 4¹/₂" including seam allowances.

9. For **Star Center**, sew 1 gold **triangle** to 2 opposite sides of green **medium square** (Fig. 5). Press seam allowances to triangles. Sew remaining triangles to medium square to make **Star Center**. Press seam allowances to triangles. Star Center should measure 4¹/₂" x 4¹/₂" including seam allowances.

10. For 2 matching **Triangle-Squares**, match right sides and place 1 cream **small square** on top of 1 red **small square**. Stitch ¹/₄" from each side of drawn line. Cut along drawn line and press seam allowances to red fabric to make 2 **Small Triangle-Squares**. Small Triangle-Square should measure 2¹/₂" x 2¹/₂" including seam allowances. Make 4 Small Triangle-Squares.

11. Sew 1 cream **very small square** and 1 **Small Triangle-Square** together to make **Unit 2**. Press seam allowances to very small square. Make 2 **Unit 2a's** and 2 **Unit 2b's**.

Fig. 1

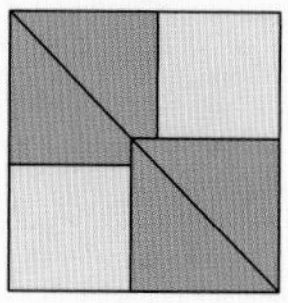

Fig. 2

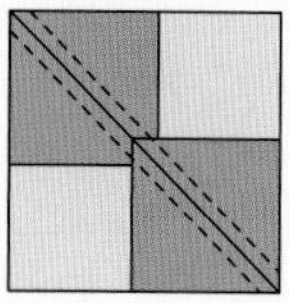

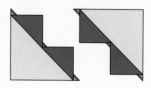
Unit 1 (make 2)

Fig. 3

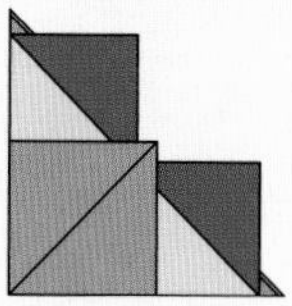

Fig. 4

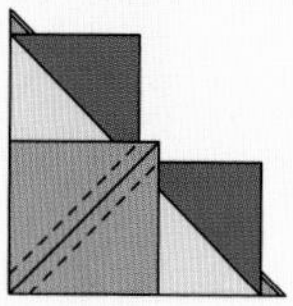

Flying Geese A (make 4)

Flying Geese B (make 4)

Fig. 5

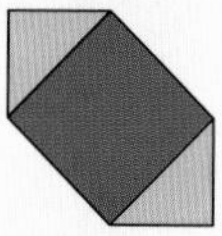

Star Center

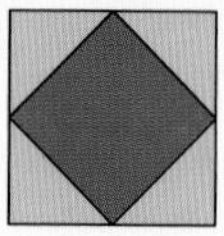

Small Triangle-Square (make 4)

Unit 2a
(make 2)

Unit 2b
(make 2)

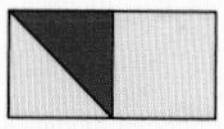

12. Sew 1 cream **rectangle** and 1 **Unit 2** together to make **Unit 3**. Press seam allowances to rectangle. Unit 3 should measure $4^1/_2$" x $4^1/_2$" including seam allowances. Make 2 Unit 3a's and 2 Unit 3b's.

13. Sew 1 **Flying Geese A** and 1 **Flying Geese B** together to make Unit 4. Press seam allowances to Flying Geese A. Unit 4 should measure $4^1/_2$" x $4^1/_2$" including seam allowances. Make 4 Unit 4's.

14. Sew 1 **Unit 3a**, 1 **Unit 3b**, and 1 **Unit 4** together to make Unit 5. Press seam allowances to Unit 3's. Make 2 Unit 5's.

15. Sew 2 **Unit 4's** and **Star Center** together to make Unit 6. Press seam allowances to Star Center.

16. Sew 2 **Unit 5's** and **Unit 6** together to make Star Block. Press seam allowances to Unit 6. Star Block should measure $12^1/_2$" x $12^1/_2$" including seam allowances.

17. Repeat Steps 1–16 to make 16 Star Blocks.

Making the Gold and Blue Triangle-Squares

1. Draw a diagonal line (corner to corner) on wrong side of each light **very large square**.

2. Place 1 light **very large square** on top of 1 gold **very large square**. Stitch $^1/_4$" from each side of drawn line. Cut along drawn line and press seam allowances to gold fabric to make 2 Gold Triangle-Squares. Gold Triangle-Square should measure $6^1/_2$" x $6^1/_2$" including seam allowances. Make 36 Gold Triangle-Squares.

3. Using cream **very large squares** and blue **very large squares**, make 44 Blue Triangle-Squares. Blue Triangle-Square should measure $6^1/_2$" x $6^1/_2$" including seam allowances.

Unit 3a
(make 2)

Unit 3b
(make 2)

Unit 4 (make 4)

Unit 5 (make 2)

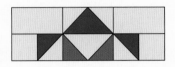

Unit 6

Star Block (make 16)

Gold Triangle-Square
(make 36)

Blue Triangle-Square
(make 44)

Making the Triangle Blocks

1. Sew 4 assorted **Gold Triangle-Squares** together to make Gold Triangle Block. Press seam allowances open or as shown by arrows (Fig. 6). Gold Triangle Block should measure $12^1/_2$" x $12^1/_2$" including seam allowances. Make 4 Gold Triangle Blocks.

2. Sew 4 assorted **Blue Triangle-Squares** together to make Blue Triangle Block. Press seam allowances open or as shown by arrows (Fig. 6). Blue Triangle Block should measure $12^1/_2$" x $12^1/_2$" including seam allowances. Make 5 Blue Triangle Blocks.

Making the Border Blocks

1. Sew 2 assorted **Gold Triangle-Squares** together to make Gold Border Block. Press seam allowances open or to one side. Gold Border Block should measure $6^1/_2$" x $12^1/_2$" including seam allowances. Make 8 Gold Border Blocks.

2. Sew 2 assorted **Blue Triangle-Squares** together to make Blue Border Block. Press seam allowances open or to one side. Blue Border Block should measure $6^1/_2$" x $12^1/_2$" including seam allowances. Make 12 Blue Border Blocks.

Assembling the Quilt Top

1. Sew 2 **Gold Triangle-Squares**, 3 **Blue Border Blocks**, and 2 **Gold Border Blocks** together to make Row A. Press seam allowances open or in one direction. Row A should measure $6^1/_2$" x $72^1/_2$" including seam allowances. Make 2 Row A's.

2. Sew 2 **Blue Border Blocks** and 5 **Star Blocks** together to make Row B. Press seam allowances open or in the opposite direction of Row A. Row B should measure $12^1/_2$" x $72^1/_2$" including seam allowances. Make 2 Row B's.

3. Sew 2 **Gold Border Blocks**, 2 **Star Blocks**, 2 **Blue Triangle Blocks**, and 1 **Gold Triangle Block** together to make Row C. Press seam allowances open or in the same direction as Row A. Row C should measure $12^1/_2$" x $72^1/_2$" including seam allowances. Make 2 **Row C's**.

Fig. 6

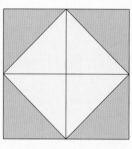

Gold Triangle Block (make 4)   **Blue Triangle Block** (make 5)

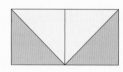 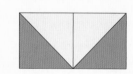

Gold Border Block (make 8)   **Blue Border Block** (make 12)

Row A (make 2)

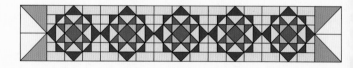

Row B (make 2)

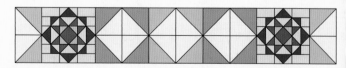

Row C (make 2)

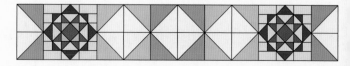

Row D

4. Sew 2 **Blue Border Blocks**, 2 **Star Blocks**, 2 **Gold Triangle Blocks**, and 1 **Blue Triangle Block** together to make Row D. Press seam allowances open or in the opposite direction of Row A. Row D should measure $12^1/2$" x $72^1/2$" including seam allowances.

5. Referring to Quilt Top Diagram, sew **Rows** together. Press seam allowances open or in one direction. Quilt top should measure $72^1/2$" x $72^1/2$" including seam allowances.

Completing the Quilt

1. To help stabilize the edges and prevent any seams from separating, stay-stitch around the quilt top approximately $1/8$" from the edge.

2. Follow **Quilting**, page 108, to mark, layer, and quilt as desired. Quilt shown was machine quilted with an all-over floral pattern.

3. Follow **Making a Hanging Sleeve**, page 109, if a hanging sleeve is desired.

4. Cut a 27" square of binding fabric. Follow **Binding**, page 110, to bind quilt using 2"w bias binding with mitered corners.

Note: You can make this quilt larger by simply adding a plain border. Or you might add a round of Triangle-Squares to the outer edges, which will make the quilt $84^1/2$" x $84^1/2$". For this, you will need an additional 28 Gold Triangle-Squares and 24 Blue Triangle-Squares.

Quilt Top Diagram

501

Quilted by Louise Haley.

Finished Quilt Size:
63¹/₂" x 75¹/₂"
(161 cm x 192 cm)

Finished Block Size:
3" x 6" (8 cm x 15 cm)

The topic was scrap quilts. The goal was to make a quilt for a class and presentation. Carrie decided to approach these fun tasks by making two quilts using the same design. The quilt named "501" came to her first, and she started with the pink floral fabric, then added blue. And of course, the blue fabric inspired the quilt's name because it reminded Carrie of vintage blue jeans like Levi's 501s. Moose Munch, page 37, is a true scrap quilt, because it started with leftover fabrics. Carrie says, "The name came to me because the red fabric came from a shop called The Quilted Moose. The fact that 'Moose Munch' is also the name of a candy made with chocolate, popcorn, and toffee —well, that's just coincidence."

Yardage Requirements

Yardage is based on 43"/44" (109 cm/112 cm) wide fabric. Fat quarters are approximately 21" x 18" (53 cm x 46 cm).

  3 yds (2.7 m) of pink print fabric
  8 fat quarters of assorted blue print fabrics (includes pieced binding)
  6 fat quarters of assorted cream print fabrics
  $4^3/_4$ yds (4.3 m) of fabric for backing

You will also need:

  72" x 84" (183 cm x 213 cm) piece of batting

Cutting Out the Pieces

*Follow **Rotary Cutting**, page 105, to cut fabric. All measurements include $^1/_4$" seam allowances. Borders are cut longer than needed and will be trimmed after assembling quilt top center.*

From pink print fabric:

- Cut 2 *lengthwise* **side outer borders** $3^1/_2$" x $73^1/_2$".
- Cut 2 *lengthwise* **top/bottom outer borders** $3^1/_2$" x $67^1/_2$".
- Cut 2 *lengthwise* **side inner borders** 2" x $64^1/_2$".
- Cut 2 *lengthwise* **top/bottom inner borders** 2" x $55^1/_2$".

From remaining width,

- Cut 20 *crosswise* strips $3^1/_2$" x 18". From these strips,
  - Cut 40 **rectangles** $3^1/_2$" x $6^1/_2$".
- Cut 7 strips $3^1/_2$" wide by the width of the fabric. From these strips,
  - Cut 36 **rectangles** $3^1/_2$" x $6^1/_2$". You will have 76 rectangles.
  - Cut 8 **squares** $3^1/_2$" x $3^1/_2$".

From *each* blue print fat quarter:

- Cut 6 **strips** 2" x 21". Cut a total of 48 **strips**.
- Cut 2 **binding strips** 2" x 21". Cut a total of 16 **binding strips**.

From *each* cream print fat quarter:

- Cut 8 **strips** 2" x 21". Cut a total of 48 **strips**.

Making the Blocks

*Follow **Piecing**, page 106, and **Pressing**, page 107, to assemble the quilt top. Because there are so many seams in this quilt, you may need to use a seam allowance slightly smaller than the usual $^1/_4$". As you sew, measure your work to compare with the measurements provided and adjust your seam allowance as needed.*

1. Sew 1 blue **strip** and 1 cream **strip** together to make **Strip Set**. Press seam allowances to blue strip. Make 48 Strip Sets. Cut across Strip Sets at 2" intervals to make 480 (240 sets of 2 matching) **Unit 1's**. Unit 1 should measure 2" x $3^1/_2$" including seam allowances.

Strip Set
(make 48)

Unit 1
(make 240 sets of 2 matching)

2. Sew 2 matching **Unit 1's** together to make **Four Patch**. To press seam allowances, follow **Collapsing the Seams**, page 107. Four Patch should measure $3^1/_2$" x $3^1/_2$" including seam allowances. Make 240 Four Patches.

Four Patch (make 240)

Tip: When placing the 2 Unit 1's together under the presser foot to make a Four Patch, turn the pieces so that the seam allowance on the top Unit 1 is facing toward the presser foot (Fig. 1). This will make your piecing consistent and will make assembling the quilt top easier.

Fig. 1

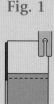

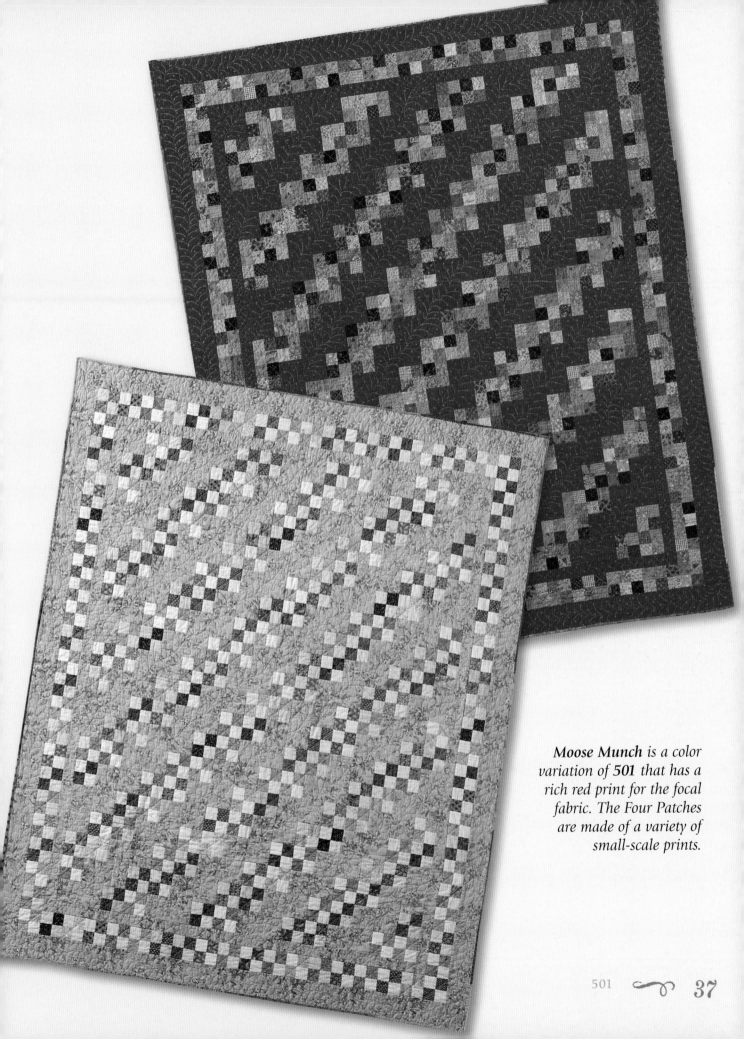

Moose Munch is a color variation of **501** that has a rich red print for the focal fabric. The Four Patches are made of a variety of small-scale prints.

3. Sew 2 **Four Patches** together to make **Block**. Press seam allowances in one direction. Block should measure $3^1/_2$" x $6^1/_2$" including seam allowances. Make 76 Blocks.

Assembling the Quilt Top Center

1. Sew 2 pink **squares**, 5 **Blocks**, and 4 pink **rectangles** together to make vertical **Row A**. Press seam allowances in one direction. Flip and re-press the seam allowances between the 2 Four Patches in each Block as needed. Row A should measure $3^1/_2$" x $60^1/_2$". Make 4 Row A's.
2. Sew 5 **Blocks** and 5 pink **rectangles** together to make vertical **Row B**. Press seam allowances in opposite direction of Row A. Row B should measure $3^1/_2$" x $60^1/_2$". Make 4 Row B's.
3. Sew 2 **Four Patches**, 5 pink **rectangles**, and 4 **Blocks** together to make **Row C**. Press seam allowances in same direction as Row A. Row C should measure $3^1/_2$" x $60^1/_2$". Make 4 Row C's.
4. Sew 5 pink **rectangles** and 5 **Blocks** together to make vertical **Row D**. Press seam allowances in opposite direction of Row A. Row D should measure $3^1/_2$" x $60^1/_2$". Make 4 Row D's.
5. Referring to **Quilt Top Diagram**, sew **Rows** together to make quilt top center. Press seam allowances in one direction. Quilt top center should measure $48^1/_2$" x $60^1/_2$".

Making the Middle Border

1. Sew 21 **Four Patches** together to make **side middle border**. Press seam allowances in one direction. Make 2 side middle borders.
2. Sew 19 **Four Patches** together to make **top/bottom middle border**. Press seam allowances in one direction. Make 2 top/bottom middle borders.
3. Set middle borders aside.

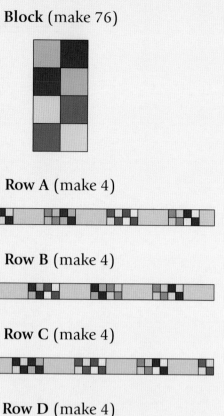

Block (make 76)

Row A (make 4)

Row B (make 4)

Row C (make 4)

Row D (make 4)

Adding the Borders

1. Measure *length* across center of quilt top center. Trim **side inner borders** to determined measurement. Matching centers and corners, sew side inner borders to quilt top center.
2. Measure *width* across center of quilt top center (including added borders). Trim **top/bottom inner borders** to determined measurement. Matching centers and corners, sew top/bottom inner borders to quilt top center.
3. Measure *length* across center of quilt top. Measure length of **side middle borders**. If measurements are not the same, make seams in borders slightly larger or smaller as needed. Matching centers and corners, sew side middle borders to quilt top.
4. Measure *width* across center of quilt top (including added borders). Measure length of **top/bottom middle borders**. If measurements are not the same, make seams in borders slightly larger or smaller as needed. Matching centers and corners, sew top/bottom middle borders to quilt top.
5. In the same manner as inner borders, add **side** and then **top** and **bottom outer borders** to quilt top. Quilt top should measure $63^1/_2$" x $75^1/_2$" including seam allowances.

Completing the Quilt

1. Follow **Quilting**, page 108, to mark, layer, and quilt as desired. Quilt shown was machine quilted. A feather pattern was quilted in the pink squares and rectangles and in the outer border. The Four Patches were diagonally cross-hatch quilted, and the inner border was quilted with a loop pattern.
2. Follow **Making a Hanging Sleeve**, page 109, if a hanging sleeve is desired.
3. Using diagonal seams, **Fig. 2**, sew binding strips together to make approximately 8 yds of 2"w straight-grain pieced binding. Follow **Attaching Binding with Mitered Corners**, page 111, to bind quilt.

Quilt Top Diagram

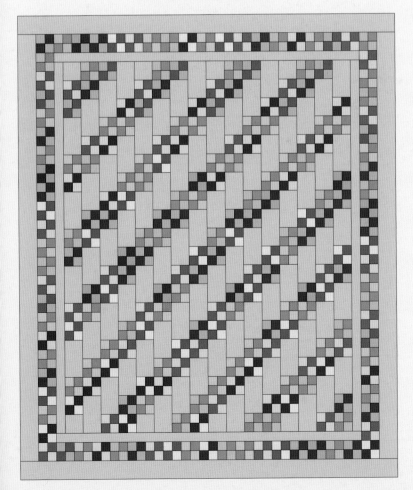

Fig. 2

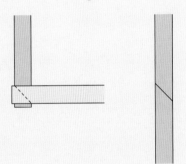

Note: By adding or subtracting a single vertical Row, you will change the width by 3". The length can be increased by 3" by adding 1 Four Patch or pink square, or changing a pink square to a pink rectangle at the bottom of each vertical Row.

The quilt can be made any size by adding or subtracting Rows and making the Rows longer or shorter—just be sure to follow the overall zigzag design and adjust the borders as needed.

Open Door

Quilted by Louise Haley.

Finished Quilt Size:
76¹/₂" x 76¹/₂"
(194 cm x 194 cm)

Finished Block Size:
20" x 20" (51 cm x 51 cm)

Carrie realized the reds and browns in this particular fabric line were pretty strong, so she wanted to be careful of their placement. She also wanted this quilt to have a "loose" look to it, so while the elements look planned, the quilt isn't overly formal. The name of a quilt is always important to Carrie. "Shangri-La, which was the name of the fabric collection, means a place of peace, happiness or bliss," she says. "Which reminded me of a favorite quote from American author and philosopher, Joseph Campbell. 'Follow your bliss and the universe will open doors for you where once there were only walls.' That quote is on the back of my quilt."

Yardage Requirements

Yardage is based on 43"/44" (109 cm/112 cm) wide fabric. Fat quarters are approximately 21" x 18" (53 cm x 46 cm).

 3 fat quarters of assorted cream print fabrics for small Triangle-Squares

 9 fat quarters of assorted light print fabrics for Blocks

 3 fat quarters of assorted large print fabrics for Block centers

 9 fat quarters of assorted dark print fabrics for Blocks

 9 fat quarters of assorted aqua print fabrics for Blocks

 9 fat quarters of assorted green print fabrics for sashings

 $^7/_8$ yd (80 cm) of fabric for binding

 $7^1/_8$ yds (6.5 m) of fabric for backing

You will also need:

 85" x 85" (216 cm x 216 cm) piece of batting

Cutting Out the Pieces

Follow **Rotary Cutting***, page 105, to cut fabric. All measurements include* $^1/_4$" *seam allowances*

From *each* assorted cream print fat quarter:

- Cut 5 strips $2^3/_8$" x 21". From these strips,
  - Cut 36 **small squares** $2^3/_8$" x $2^3/_8$". Cut a total of 108 (9 sets of 12 matching) small squares.
- Cut 2 strips 2" x 21". From these strips,
  - Cut 12 **very small squares** 2" x 2". Cut a total of 36 (9 sets of 4 matching) very small squares.

From *each* assorted light print fat quarter:

- Cut 1 strip $9^1/_4$" x 21". From this strip,
  - Cut 1 **very large square** $9^1/_4$" x $9^1/_4$". Cut a total of 9 very large squares.

  From remainder of strip,
  - Cut 1 strip $5^3/_8$" x $11^3/_4$". From this strip,
    - Cut 2 **large squares** $5^3/_8$" x $5^3/_8$". Cut a total of 18 (9 sets of 2 matching) large squares.
- Cut 1 strip $2^1/_2$" x 21". From this strip,
  - Cut 4 **medium squares** $2^1/_2$" x $2^1/_2$". Cut a total of 32 medium squares.

From *each* assorted large print fat quarter:

- Cut 2 strips $8^1/_2$" x 21". From these strips,
  - Cut 3 **center squares** $8^1/_2$" x $8^1/_2$". Cut a total of 9 center squares.

From *each* assorted dark print fat quarter:

- Cut 1 strip $9^1/_4$" x 21". From this strip,
  - Cut 1 **very large square** $9^1/_4$" x $9^1/_4$". Cut a total of 9 very large squares.

  From remainder of strip,
  - Cut 3 strips $2^3/_8$" x $11^3/_4$". From these strips,
    - Cut 12 **small squares** $2^3/_8$" x $2^3/_8$". Cut a total of 108 (9 sets of 12 matching) small squares.
- Cut 1 strip $2^1/_2$" x 21". From this strip,
  - Cut 4 **medium squares** $2^1/_2$" x $2^1/_2$". Cut a total of 36 (9 sets of 4 matching) medium squares.

From *each* assorted aqua print fat quarter:

- Cut 1 strip $9^1/_4$" x 21". From this strip,
  - Cut 2 **very large squares** $9^1/_4$" x $9^1/_4$". Cut a total of 18 (9 sets of 2 matching) very large squares.
- Cut 1 strip $5^3/_8$" x 21". From this strip,
  - Cut 2 **large squares** $5^3/_8$" x $5^3/_8$". Cut a total of 18 (9 sets of 2 matching) large squares.

  From remainder of strip,
  - Cut 1 strip $2^1/_2$" x $10^1/_4$". From this strip,
    - Cut 4 **medium squares** $2^1/_2$" x $2^1/_2$". Cut a total of 32 medium squares.

From *each* assorted green print fat quarter:

- Cut 1 strip $10^1/_2$" x 21". From this strip,
  - Cut 4 *lengthwise* rectangles $4^1/_2$" x $10^1/_2$". Cut a total of 36 *lengthwise* rectangles.
- Cut 1 strip $4^1/_2$" x 21". From this strip,
  - Cut 2 *crosswise* rectangles $4^1/_2$" x $10^1/_2$". Cut a total of 12 *crosswise* rectangles.

Note: *Set aside 24 of the lengthwise rectangles for the sashings along the outer edges of the quilt top for added stability.*

Making the Blocks

Selecting Pieces for the Blocks

1. Select the following pieces for each Block.

From 1 cream print:
  12 **small squares** and
  4 **very small squares**.

From 1 light print:
  1 **very large square** and
  2 **large squares**.

From 1 large print fat quarter:
  1 **center square**.

From 1 dark print:
  1 **very large square**,
  4 **medium squares**, and
  12 **small squares**.

From 1 aqua print:
Note: Quilt shown has 1 Block with assorted aqua prints.
  2 **very large squares** and
  2 **large squares**.

Making the Triangle-Squares

*Follow **Piecing**, page 106, and **Pressing**, page 107, to assemble the quilt top. Because there are so many seams in this quilt, you may need to use a seam allowance slightly smaller than the usual* $1/4"$. *As you sew, measure your work to compare with the measurements provided and adjust your seam allowance as needed.* **Note:** *Use pieces for 1 Block throughout for Block construction.*

1. Draw a diagonal line (corner to corner) on wrong side of each cream **small square** and each light **large square**.

2. Matching right sides, place 1 cream **small square** on top of 1 dark **small square**. Stitch $1/4"$ from each side of drawn line (Fig. 1). Cut along drawn line and press seam allowances to dark fabric to make 2 Small Triangle-Squares. Small Triangle-Square should measure 2" x 2" including seam allowances. Make 24 matching Small Triangle-Squares.

3. Use light **large square** and aqua **large square** to make 2 Large Triangle-Squares. Press seam allowances to aqua fabric. Large Triangle-Square should measure 5" x 5" including seam allowances. Make 4 matching Large Triangle-Squares.

4. Repeat Steps 1–3 to make 24 matching Small Triangles-Squares and 4 matching Large Triangle-Squares for each Block.

Making the Hourglasses

1. Draw a diagonal line (corner to corner) on wrong side of each aqua **very large square**.

2. Matching right sides, place 1 aqua **very large square** on top of dark **very large square**. Stitch $1/4"$ from each side of drawn line. Cut along drawn line and press seam allowances to aqua fabric to make 2 Dark Triangle-Squares. Dark Triangle-Square should measure $8^7/8"$ x $8^7/8"$ including seam allowances.

3. Use remaining aqua **very large square** and light **very large square** to make 2 Light Triangle-Squares. Press seam allowances to aqua fabric. Light Triangle-Square should measure $8^7/8"$ x $8^7/8"$ including seam allowances.

Fig. 1

Small Triangle-Square
(make 24 matching)

Large Triangle-Square
(make 4 matching)

Dark Triangle-Square
(make 2)

Light Triangle-Square
(make 2)

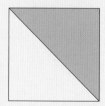

4. On wrong side of each **Light Triangle-Square**, draw a diagonal line (corner to corner and perpendicular to seam).
5. Matching right sides and seams, place 1 **Light Triangle-Square** on top of 1 **Dark Triangle-Square** with aqua triangles opposite each other. Stitch $1/4$" from each side of drawn line (Fig. 2). Cut apart along drawn line to make 2 Hourglasses. Press seam allowances to one side. Hourglass should measure $8^1/2$" x $8^1/2$" including seam allowances. Make 4 matching Hourglasses.
6. Trim 2" from each Hourglass *on dark triangle side* (Fig. 3) to make 4 Unit 1's. Unit 1 should measure $8^1/2$" x $6^1/2$".
7. Repeat Steps 1–6 to make 4 matching Unit 1's for each Block.

Making the Snowballs

1. Draw a diagonal line (corner to corner) on the wrong side of each dark **medium square**.
2. With right sides together, place 1 dark **medium square** on 1 corner of **center square** and stitch along drawn line (Fig. 4). Trim $1/4$" from stitching line (Fig. 5). Open up and press seam allowances toward triangle.
3. In the same manner, sew dark medium squares to remaining corners of center square to make Snowball. Snowball should measure $8^1/2$" x $8^1/2$" including seam allowances.
4. Repeat Steps 1–3 to make 1 Snowball for each Block.

Making the Corner Units

Press seam allowances open or as indicated by arrows in diagrams.

1. Sew 3 **Small Triangle-Squares** together to make Unit 2. Make 4 matching Unit 2's.
2. Sew 3 **Small Triangle-Squares** and 1 cream **very small square** together to make Unit 3. Make 4 matching Unit 3's.

Fig. 2

Hourglass
(make 4 matching)

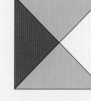

Fig. 3

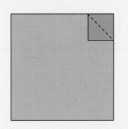

2"

Unit 1
(make 4 matching)

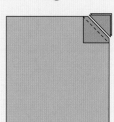

Fig. 4

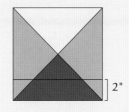

Fig. 5

Snowball

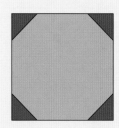

Unit 2
(make 4 matching)

Unit 3
(make 4 matching)

3. Sew 1 **Unit 2** and 1 **Large Triangle-Square** together to make Unit 4. Make 4 matching Unit 4's.
4. Sew 1 **Unit 3** and 1 **Unit 4** together to make Corner Unit. Corner Unit should measure $6^1/_2$" x $6^1/_2$" including seam allowances. Make 4 matching Corner Units.
5. Repeat Steps 1–4 to make 4 matching Corner Units for each Block.

Assembling the Blocks

1. Sew 2 **Corner Units** and 1 **Unit 1** together to make Unit 5. Press seam allowances to Unit 1. Make 2 matching Unit 5's.
2. Sew 2 matching **Unit 1's** and 1 **Snowball** together to make Unit 6. Press seam allowances to Unit 1's.
3. Sew 2 **Unit 5's** and **Unit 6** together to make Block. Press seam allowances to Unit 6. Block should measure $20^1/_2$" x $20^1/_2$" including seam allowances.
4. Repeat Steps 1–3 to make 9 Blocks.

Making the Sashings

1. Sew 2 **lengthwise rectangles** together to make outer sashing strip. Press seam allowances to 1 side or press them open. Outer sashing strip should measure $4^1/_2$" x $20^1/_2$" including seam allowances. Make 12 outer sashing strips.
2. Using remaining rectangles, sew 2 **rectangles** together to make inner sashing strip. Press seam allowances to 1 side or press them open. Inner sashing strip should measure $4^1/_2$" x $20^1/_2$" including seam allowances. Make 12 inner sashing strips.
3. Sew 1 light **medium square** and 1 aqua **medium square** together to make Unit 7. Press seam allowances to aqua print. Make 32 Unit 7's.
4. Sew 2 **Unit 7's** together to make Four Patch. To press seam allowances, follow **Collapsing the Seams**, page 107. Four Patch should measure $4^1/_2$" x $4^1/_2$" including seam allowances. Make 16 Four Patches.

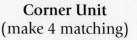

Unit 4
(make 4 matching)

Corner Unit
(make 4 matching)

Unit 5 (make 2 matching)

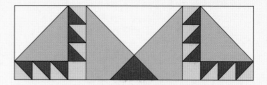

Unit 6

Block (make 9)

Outer Sashing Strip (make 12)

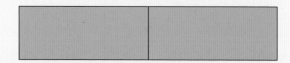

Inner Sashing Strip (make 12)

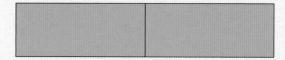

Assembling the Quilt Top

1. Sew 4 **Four Patches** and 3 **outer sashing strips** together to make Outer Sashing Row. Press seam allowances to outer sashing strips. Outer Sashing Row should measure 76$\frac{1}{2}$" x 4$\frac{1}{2}$" including seam allowances. Make 2 Outer Sashing Rows.
2. Sew 4 **Four Patches** and 3 **inner sashing strips** together to make Inner Sashing Row. Press seam allowances to inner sashing strips. Inner Sashing Row should measure 76$\frac{1}{2}$" x 4$\frac{1}{2}$" including seam allowances. Make 2 Inner Sashing Rows.
3. Sew 3 **Blocks**, 2 **inner sashing strips**, and 2 **outer sashing strips** together to make Block Row. Press seam allowances to sashing strips. Block Row should measure 76$\frac{1}{2}$" x 20$\frac{1}{2}$" including seam allowances. Make 3 Block Rows.
4. Referring to Quilt Top Diagram, sew **Rows** together to complete quilt top. Quilt top should measure 76$\frac{1}{2}$" x 76$\frac{1}{2}$" including seam allowances.

Completing the Quilt

1. To help stabilize the edges and prevent any seams from separating, stay-stitch around the quilt top approximately $\frac{1}{8}$" from the edge.
2. Follow **Quilting**, page 108, to mark, layer, and quilt as desired. Quilt shown was machine quilted. Feather patterns were quilted in the Snowballs, aqua areas of the Blocks, and sashing strips. The cream and light areas of the Blocks were stipple quilted. Squares with curved sides were quilted in each square of the Four Patches.
3. Follow **Making a Hanging Sleeve**, page 109, if a hanging sleeve is desired.
4. Cut a 27" square of binding fabric. Follow **Binding**, page 110, to bind quilt using 2"w bias binding with mitered corners.

Note: This quilt can be made smaller or larger by subtracting or adding Blocks to the length or width. Subtracting or adding a single Row or Column will change the measurement by 24".

For a slightly larger quilt, a plain border may be added.

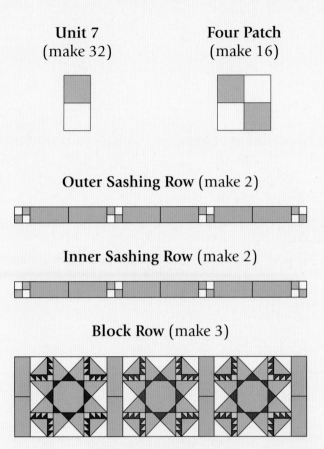

Unit 7 (make 32)

Four Patch (make 16)

Outer Sashing Row (make 2)

Inner Sashing Row (make 2)

Block Row (make 3)

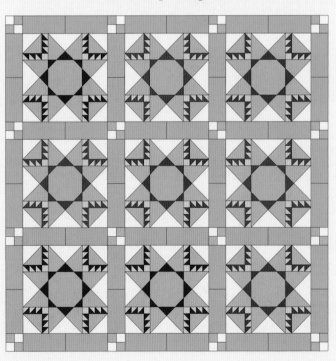

Quilt Top Diagram

Going Buggy

Quilted by Diane Tricka.

Finished Quilt Size:
74¹/₂" x 74¹/₂"
(189 cm x 189 cm)

Finished Block Size:
8" x 8" (20 cm x 20 cm)

Curved pieces in quilts—they're not usually every quilter's idea of something fun to make—but wait until you see the clever way Carrie made these curvy blocks! Instead of sewing curved seams, she uses invisible machine appliqué to sew whole circles, which are then cut into quarters. Dogwood Blossom is the traditional name for the large block that Carrie saw on an antique two-color quilt. Of course Carrie wanted to use "way more than two colors," and she thought she might as well break up the large traditional block into four segments to make two each of light and dark. The unusual name for this quilt came from Carrie's trip to a shop named Buggy Barn Quilts.

Yardage Requirements

Yardage is based on 43"/44" (109 cm/112 cm) wide fabric. Fat quarters are approximately 21" x 18" (53 cm x 46 cm).

16 fat quarters of assorted light print fabrics

23 fat quarters of assorted dark print fabrics

$^7/_8$ yd (80 cm) of fabric for binding

7 yds (6.4 m)* of fabric for backing

You will also need:

83" x 83" (211 cm x 211 cm) piece of batting

Freezer paper

Water-soluble fabric glue stick

Clear or smoke monofilament thread

Stabilizer

*Yardage is based on 3 lengths of fabric, which allows for a larger backing for long arm quilting. If you are using another quilting method, 2 lengths or $4^5/_8$ yds (4.2 m) will be adequate.

Cutting Out the Pieces

Follow **Rotary Cutting**, page 105, to cut fabric. All measurements include $^1/_4$" seam allowances.

From *each* assorted light print fat quarter:

- Cut 1 strip 9" x 21". From this strip,
  - Cut 2 **large squares** 9" x 9". Cut a total of 32 large squares.
- Cut 2 **strips** $2^1/_2$" x 21". Cut a total of 32 strips.
- Cut 1 **border strip** $1^1/_2$" x 21". Cut a total of 16 border strips.

From *each* assorted dark print fabrics:

- Cut 3 **strips** $2^1/_2$" x 21". Cut a total of 68 strips.
- Cut 2 **large squares** 9" x 9". Cut a total of 32 large squares.

Making the Four Patches

Follow **Piecing**, page 106, and **Pressing**, page 107, to assemble the quilt top. Because there are so many seams in this quilt, you may need to use a seam allowance slightly smaller than the usual $^1/_4$". As you sew, measure your work to compare with the measurements provided and adjust your seam allowance as needed.

1. Sew 1 light **strip** and 1 dark **strip** together to make **Strip Set A**. Press seam allowances to dark strip. Make 32 Strip Set A's. Cut across Strip Set A's at $2^1/_2$" intervals to make 256 **Unit 1's**. Unit 1 should measure $2^1/_2$" x $4^1/_2$" including seam allowances.

2. Sew 2 **Unit 1's** together to make **Four Patch**. To press seam allowances, follow **Collapsing the Seams**, page 107. Four Patch should measure $4^1/_2$" x $4^1/_2$" including seam allowances. Make 128 Four Patches.

Strip Set A
(make 32)

Unit 1
(make 256)

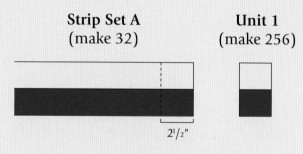

$2^1/_2$"

Four Patch (make 128)

Making the Quarter-Circle Squares

*Follow **Invisible Applique**, page 107, and use circle patterns, page 55, to make the **Circle Squares**.*

1. Trace 32 large circles and 32 small circles onto dull side of freezer paper; cut out.
2. Using a dry iron, center and iron 1 freezer paper large circle, shiny side down, on wrong side of 1 dark **large square**. Trim **large square** 1/4" outside edge of freezer paper circle.
3. Apply a very thin and narrow layer of glue around edge of freezer paper circle. Use fingers to fold and smooth fabric edge over freezer paper circle (**Fig. 1**).

Fig. 1

Fig. 2

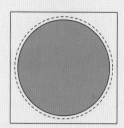

Unit 2a
(make 16)

Circle Square A
(make 16)

Unit 2b
(make 16)

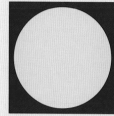

Circle Square B
(make 16)

Fig. 3

Quarter-Circle
Square A (make 64)

Quarter-Circle
Square B (make 64)

Tip: For Invisible Appliqué, use a 70/10 or 60/8 sewing machine needle, clear or smoke monofilament thread in the needle, and a 50 or 60 wt. thread in the bobbin.

4. With right sides facing up, center fabric/ freezer paper circle on 1 light **large square**; pin. Appliqué circle to large square to make **Unit 2a**. Carefully cut away fabric behind appliquéd circle $^1/_4$" inside stitching line (**Fig. 2**). Cut-out piece will be used later for small circle appliqué.

5. Remove the freezer paper circle from the wrong side of the appliqué. Use a spray bottle to dampen edges to remove glue if necessary.

6. Repeat Steps 2–5 to make a total of 16 Unit 2a's.

7. Using light **large squares** to make circle appliqués and dark **large squares** for backgrounds, repeat Steps 2–5 to make a total of 16 **Unit 2b**'s.

8. Using the cut-out pieces from Step 4 and small freezer paper circles, appliqué 1 light small circle to each **Unit 2a** to make 16 **Circle Square A**'s. Appliqué 1 dark small circle to each **Unit 2b** to make 16 **Circle Square B**'s. Carefully cut away fabric behind appliquéd small circles $^1/_4$" inside stitching line.

9. Use ruler and rotary cutter to cut each Circle Square into four $4^1/_2$"x $4^1/_2$" **Quarter-Circle Squares** (**Fig. 3**). Make 64 **Quarter-Circle Square A**'s and 64 **Quarter-Circle Square B**'s.

Making the Blocks

1. For each **Block A**, select 2 **Four Patches** and 2 **Quarter-Circle Square A's**.

2. Sew 1 **Four Patch** and 1 **Quarter-Circle Square A** together to make **Unit 3**. Press seam allowances to Four Patches. Make 2 Unit 3's.

3. Sew 2 **Unit 3's** together to make **Block A**. To press seam allowances, follow **Collapsing the Seams**, page 107. Block A should measure $8^1/_2$" x $8^1/_2$" including seam allowances.

4. Repeat Steps 1–3 to make 32 **Block A's**.
5. Using **Quarter-Circle Square B's**, repeat Steps 1–3 to make 32 **Block B's**. **Block B** should measure 8¹/₂" x 8¹/₂" including seam allowance.

Assembling the Quilt Top Center

1. Sew 4 **Block A's** and 4 **Block B's** together to make **Row**. Press seam allowances open or in one direction. Row should measure 8¹/₂" x 64¹/₂" including seam allowances. Make 8 Rows.
2. Referring to **Quilt Top Diagram**, page 54, and rotating every other Row, sew **Rows** together to make quilt top center. Press seam allowances open or in one direction. Quilt top center should measure 64¹/₂" x 64¹/₂" including seam allowances.

Adding the Inner Border

1. Using diagonal seams (**Fig. 4**), sew **border strips** together into a continuous strip approximately 7³/₄ yds long. Press seam allowances open.
2. To determine length of **side inner borders**, measure *length* across center of quilt top center. Cut 2 side inner borders from continuous strip. Matching centers and corners, sew side inner borders to quilt top center.
3. To determine length of **top/bottom inner borders**, measure width across center of quilt top center (including added borders). Cut 2 top/bottom inner borders from continuous strip. Matching centers and corners, sew top/bottom inner borders to quilt top center.

Adding the Outer Border

1. Sew 2 dark **strips** together to make **Strip Set B**. Make 18 Strip Set B's. Press seam allowances to one side. Cut across Strip Set B's at 2¹/₂" intervals to make 140 **Unit 4's**. Unit 4 should measure 2¹/₂" x 4¹/₂" including seam allowances.
2. Sew 33 **Unit 4's** together to make **side outer border**. Press seam allowances open or in one direction. Make 2 side outer borders. Measure *length* across center of quilt top. Measure length of side outer borders. If measurements are not the same, make seams in borders slightly larger or smaller as needed. Matching centers and corners, sew side outer borders to quilt top.

Unit 3 (make 2)

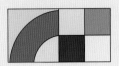

Block A (make 32) **Block B** (make 32)

Row

Fig. 4

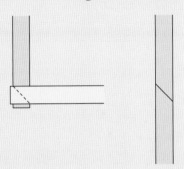

Strip Set B (make 18) **Unit 4** (make 140)

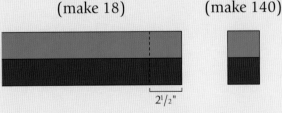

2¹/₂"

Side Outer Border (make 2)

3. Sew 37 **Unit 4's** together to make **top outer border**. Press seam allowances open or in one direction. Repeat to make **bottom outer border**. Measure *width* across center of quilt top. Measure length of top/bottom outer borders. If measurements are not the same, make seams in borders slightly larger or smaller as needed. Matching centers and corners, sew top/bottom outer borders to quilt top center.

Top/Bottom Outer Border (make 2)

Completing the Quilt

1. To help stabilize the edges and prevent any seams from separating, stay-stitch around the quilt top approximately $1/8$" from the edge.
2. Follow **Quilting**, page 108, to mark, layer, and quilt as desired. Quilt shown was machine quilted. The Blocks were quilted in the ditch around the outer edges and around the Four Patches and Quarter-Circle Squares. A repeat pattern of arches and leaves was quilted in the Blocks. The inner border was quilted in the ditch and with a continuous loop pattern. The outer border was quilted with overlapping arches.
3. Follow **Making a Hanging Sleeve**, page 109, if a hanging sleeve is desired.
4. Cut a 27" square of binding fabric. Follow **Binding**, page 110, to bind quilt using 2"w bias binding with mitered corners.

Quilt Top Diagram

Small Circle Pattern

1/2 Large Circle Pattern

*With dull side out, fold a
piece of freezer paper in half.
Align fold with straight line
and trace half circle. Cut out
along drawn line and open
for full circle.*

*Note: This quilt can be made smaller or larger
by subtracting or adding Blocks to the length or
width. To maintain the symmetry of the design,
2 Blocks should be added to the length or
width, changing the measurement by 16".*

*You may also add more Rows of small squares
to the scrappy border or add additional plain
borders.*

Home Sweet Home

Quilted by Sharon Brooks.

Finished Quilt Size:
78¹/₂" x 78¹/₂"
(199 cm x 199 cm)

Finished Block Size:
18" x 18" (46 cm x 46 cm)

This quilt came about because
Carrie needed to create a design
suitable for a quilt retreat. In trying
to do something new—something that
would be fun to make and wouldn't
require a lifetime commitment to
finish—this springtime beauty is what
Carrie came up with. "Home Sweet
Home appeals to our need for nesting,"
says Carrie. "We all like to surround
ourselves with things we love and that
make us happy. For me, as a quilter,
that means using blocks and fabrics
that I love. Nine Patches, House
Blocks, Flying Geese and…okay, there
aren't any stars in this quilt, but
three out of four works for me." Most
of the fabrics were from a line called
Sweet Romance, so the name of the
quilt was just a natural.

57

Yardage Requirements

Yardage is based on 43"/44" (109 cm/112 cm) wide fabric. Fat quarters are approximately 21" x 18" (53 cm x 46 cm).

- 12 fat quarters of assorted cream print fabrics
- 7 fat quarters of assorted pink print fabrics
- 6 fat quarters of assorted blue print fabrics
- 6 fat quarters of assorted green print fabrics
- 12 fat quarters of assorted yellow print fabrics
- $7/8$ yd (80 cm) of fabric for binding
- $7^1/4$ yds (6.6 m) of fabric for backing

You will also need:

- 87" x 87" (221 cm x 221 cm) piece of batting

Cutting Out the Pieces

*Follow **Rotary Cutting**, page 105, to cut fabric. All measurements include $1/4$" seam allowances.*

FOR HOUSE BLOCK

From 1 cream print fat quarter:
- Cut 6 strips $1^1/2$" x 21". From these strips,
  - Cut 4 **large background rectangles** $1^1/2$" x $16^1/2$".
  - Cut 2 **small background rectangles** $1^1/2$" x $10^1/2$".
  - Cut 2 **small background squares** $1^1/2$" x $1^1/2$".
- Cut 1 **background strip** 2" x 21".
- Cut 1 strip $3^1/2$" x 21". From this strip,
  - Cut 2 **large background squares** $3^1/2$" x $3^1/2$".

From 1 pink print fat quarter:
- Cut 1 strip $3^1/2$" x 21". From this strip,
  - Cut 1 **roof** $3^1/2$" x $16^1/2$".

From a 2nd pink print fat quarter:
- Cut 1 strip 3" x 21". From this strip,
  - Cut 1 **door** 3" x $4^1/2$".

From *each* blue print fat quarter:
- Cut 2 **siding strips** $1^1/2$" x 21". Cut a total of 10 **siding strips**.

From 1 green print fat quarter:
- Cut 1 strip 2" x 21". From this strip,
  - Cut 2 **grass rectangles** 2" x $7^1/4$".

From a 2nd green print fat quarter:
- Cut 1 strip 2" x 21". From this strip,
  - Cut 2 **chimneys** 2" x 2".

From 1 yellow print fat quarter:
- Cut 1 strip $2^1/2$" x 21". From this strip,
- Cut 9 **windows** $2^1/2$" x $1^3/4$".

From a 2nd yellow print fat quarter:
- Cut 1 strip 2" x 21". From this strip,
- Cut 1 **path** 2" x 6".

From a 3rd yellow print fat quarter:
- Cut 1 strip $1^1/2$" x 21". From this strip,
- Cut 4 **corner squares** $1^1/2$" x $1^1/2$".

FOR REMAINDER OF QUILT TOP

From *each* of remaining 11 cream print fat quarters:
- Cut 4 strips $2^7/8$" x 21". From these strips,
  - Cut 24 **small squares** $2^7/8$" x $2^7/8$". Cut a total of 248 (54 sets of 4 matching and 16 sets of 2 matching) small squares.
- Cut 2 strips $2^1/2$" x 21". From these strips,
  - Cut 16 **very small squares** $2^1/2$" x $2^1/2$". Cut a total of 160 (40 sets of 4 matching) very small squares.

From *each* of 6 pink print fat quarters:
- Cut 1 strip $5^1/4$" x 21". From this strip,
  - Cut 3 **large squares** $5^1/4$" x $5^1/4$". Cut a total of 18 large squares.
- Cut 2 strips $2^1/2$" x 21". From these strips,
  - Cut 10 **very small squares** $2^1/2$" x $2^1/2$". Cut a total of 60 (12 sets of 5 matching) very small squares.

From remaining pink print fat quarter:
- Cut 3 strips $3^5/16$" x 21". From these strips,
  - Cut 16 **medium squares** $3^5/16$" x $3^5/16$". *(Note: $3^5/16$" is halfway between the $3^1/4$" and $3^3/8$" marks on your ruler.)*

From *each* blue print fat quarter:
- Cut 1 strip $5^1/4$" x 21". From this strip,
  - Cut 3 **large squares** $5^1/4$" x $5^1/4$". Cut a total of 18 large squares.
- Cut 2 strips $2^1/2$" x 21". From these strips,
  - Cut 15 **very small squares** $2^1/2$" x $2^1/2$". Cut a total of 70 (14 sets of 5 matching) very small squares.

From *each* green print fat quarter:

- Cut 1 strip 5$\frac{1}{4}$" x 21". From this strip,
  - Cut 3 **large squares** 5$\frac{1}{4}$" x 5$\frac{1}{4}$". Cut a total of 18 **large squares**.
- Cut 2 strips 2$\frac{1}{2}$" x 21". From these strips,
  - Cut 15 **very small squares** 2$\frac{1}{2}$" x 2$\frac{1}{2}$". Cut a total of 70 (14 sets of 5 matching) very small squares.

From *each* yellow print fat quarter:

- Cut 2 **border strips** 4$\frac{1}{2}$" x 21". Cut a total of 20 border strips.
- Cut 1 strip 6$\frac{1}{2}$" x 21". From this strip,
  - Cut 3 **very large squares** 6$\frac{1}{2}$" x 6$\frac{1}{2}$". Cut a total of 32 very large squares.

home sweet home

Making the House Block

Follow **Piecing**, page 106, and **Pressing**, page 107, to assemble the quilt top. Because there are so many seams in this quilt, you may need to use a seam allowance slightly smaller than the usual $1/4$". As you sew, measure your work to compare with the measurements provided and adjust your seam allowance as needed.

House Front Unit

1. Arrange the 10 blue **siding strips** in the order you wish them to appear and number each from top to bottom.
2. Sew pairs of **siding strips** together, working from top to bottom, to make 5 Siding Units. Press seam allowances to odd numbered siding strips.
3. For Top Siding Unit, trim **Siding Unit 1/2** to $14^1/2$" x $2^1/2$".
4. Cut **Siding Unit 3/4** into 2 **end segments** of $1^7/8$" x $2^1/2$" and 4 **inner segments** of $1^3/4$" x $2^1/2$". Sew these **end** and **inner segments** and 5 **windows** together to make Top Window Unit. Press seam allowances to windows. Top Window Unit should measure $14^1/2$" x $2^1/2$" including seam allowances.
5. For Middle Siding Unit, trim **Siding Unit 5/6** to $14^1/2$" x $2^1/2$".
6. Cut **Siding Unit 7/8** into 4 **end segments** of $1^5/8$" x $2^1/2$" and 2 **inner segments** of $1^1/2$" x $2^1/2$". Sew 2 **end segments**, 1 **inner segment**, and 2 **windows** together to make Bottom Window Unit. Press seam allowances to windows. Bottom Window Unit should measure $6^1/4$" x $2^1/2$" including seam allowances. Make 2 Bottom Window Units.
7. From **Siding Unit 9/10**, cut 2 Bottom Siding Units $6^1/4$" x $2^1/2$".
8. Sew 1 **Bottom Window Unit** and 1 **Bottom Siding Unit** together to make Bottom House Unit. Press seam allowances in one direction. Bottom House Unit should measure $6^1/4$" x $4^1/2$" including seam allowances. Make 2 Bottom House Units.
9. Sew 2 **Bottom House Units** and **door** together to make Door Unit. Press seam allowances to door. Door Unit should measure $14^1/2$" x $4^1/2$" including seam allowances.
10. Sew **Top Siding Unit**, **Top Window Unit**, **Middle Siding Unit**, and **Door Unit** together to make House Front Unit. Press seam allowances in one direction. House Front Unit should measure $14^1/2$" x $10^1/2$" including seam allowances.

Siding Unit (make 5)

Top Siding Unit

Top Window Unit

Middle Siding Unit

Bottom Window Unit (make 2)

Bottom Siding Unit (make 2)

Bottom House Unit (make 2)

Door Unit

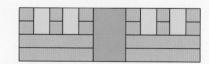

House Front Unit

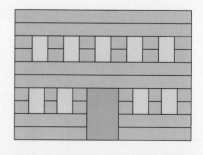

House Top Unit

1. Draw a diagonal line (corner to corner) on wrong side each **large background square**.
2. With right sides together and making sure drawn lines are turned correctly, place 1 **large background square** on each end of **roof** (Fig. 1).
3. Stitch along drawn lines and trim seam allowances to ¹/₄" (Fig. 2) to make Roof Unit. Press seam allowances to triangles. Roof Unit should measure 16¹/₂" x 3¹/₂" including seam allowances.
4. Cut **background strip** into 2 **end segments** 3¹/₂" x 2" and 1 **inner segment** 7¹/₂" x 2". Sew these **end** and **inner segments** and 2 **chimneys** together to make Chimney Unit. Press seam allowances to chimneys. Chimney Unit should measure 16¹/₂" x 2" including seam allowances.
5. Sew **Roof Unit** and **Chimney Unit** together to make House Top Unit. Press seam allowances open or in one direction. House Top Unit should measure 16¹/₂" x 5" including seam allowances.

Ground Unit

1. Using the 45° line on ruler, draw a diagonal line on one end on wrong side of 1 **grass rectangle**. Draw a diagonal line in the opposite direction on remaining **grass rectangle** (Fig. 3).
2. With right sides together and making sure drawn lines are turned correctly, place 1 **grass rectangle** on each end of **path** (Fig. 4).

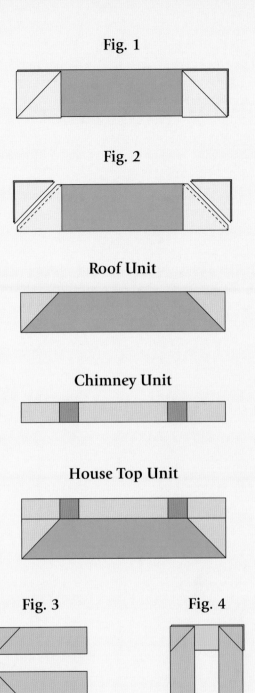

Fig. 1

Fig. 2

Roof Unit

Chimney Unit

House Top Unit

Fig. 3

Fig. 4

3. Stitch along drawn lines and trim seam allowances to ¹/₄" (Fig. 5) to make Path Unit. Press seam allowances to grass rectangles. Path Unit should measure 16¹/₂" x 2" including seam allowances.

4. Draw a diagonal line (corner to corner) on wrong side of each **small background square**.

5. With right sides together and making sure drawn lines are turned correctly, place 1 **small background square** on each end along the top edge of **Path Unit** (Fig. 6).

6. Stitch along drawn lines and trim seam allowances to ¹/₄" (Fig. 7) to make Ground Unit. Press seam allowances to triangles. Ground Unit should measure 16¹/₂" x 2" including seam allowances.

Assembling the House Block

1. Sew **House Front Unit** and 2 **small background rectangles** together to make Unit 1. Press seam allowances to background rectangles. Unit 1 should measure 16¹/₂" x 10¹/₂" including seam allowances.

2. Sew **House Top Unit**, **Unit 1**, and **Ground Unit** together to make House. Press seam allowances open or in one direction. House should measure 16¹/₂" x 16¹/₂" including seam allowances.

3. Referring to **House Block** diagram, sew 1 **large background rectangle** to each side (left and right) of **House**. Press seam allowances to rectangles.

Fig. 5

Path Unit

Fig. 6

Fig. 7

Ground Unit

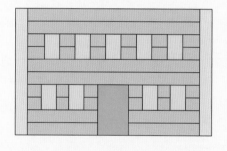

Unit 1

House

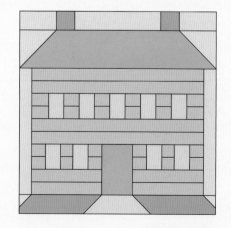

4. Sew 1 **corner square** to each end of 1 **large background rectangle** to make Unit 2. Press seam allowances to rectangle. Unit 2 should measure 18¹/₂" x 1¹/₂" including seam allowances. Make 2 Unit 2's.

5. Sew 2 **Unit 2's** and **House** together to make House Block. Press seam allowances to Unit 2's. House Block should measure 18¹/₂" x 18¹/₂" including seam allowances.

Making the Double Nine Patches

1. For 1 **Nine Patch**, select 5 matching pink, blue, or green **very small squares** and 4 matching cream **very small squares**.

2. Sew 2 pink, blue, or green **very small squares** and 1 cream **very small square** together to make Unit 3. Press seam allowances away from cream very small square. Make 2 Unit 3's.

3. Sew 2 cream **very small squares** and 1 pink, blue, or green **very small square** together to make Unit 4. Press seam allowances away from cream very small squares.

4. Sew 2 **Unit 3's** and **Unit 4** together to make Nine Patch. Press seam allowances to Unit 3's. Nine Patch should measure 6¹/₂" x 6¹/₂" including seam allowances.

5. Repeat Steps 1–4 to make a total of 40 Nine Patches.

6. Sew 2 assorted **Nine Patches** and 1 yellow **very large square** together to make Unit 5. Press seam allowances to very large square. Make 2 Unit 5's.

7. Sew 2 yellow **very large squares** and 1 **Nine Patch** (of any color) together to make Unit 6. Press seam allowances to very large squares.

Unit 2 (make 2)

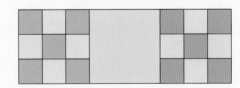

House Block

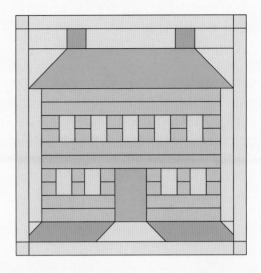

Unit 3 (make 2)　　　　**Unit 4**

Nine Patch (make 40)

Unit 5 (make 2)

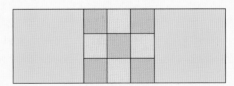

Unit 6

8. Sew 2 **Unit 5's** and **Unit 6** together to make Double Nine Patch Block. Press seam allowances to Unit 6. Double Nine Patch Block should measure 18$\frac{1}{2}$" x 18$\frac{1}{2}$" including seam allowances.

9. Repeat Steps 6–8 to make a total of 8 Double Nine Patch Blocks.

Making the Flying Geese Strips

1. Draw a diagonal line (corner to corner) on wrong side of 216 (54 sets of 4 matching) cream print **small squares**.

2. For 4 matching **Flying Geese**, select 4 matching cream **small squares** and 1 pink, blue, or green **large square**.

3. Matching right sides, place 1 **small square** on opposite corners of **large square** (Fig. 8); pin in place.

4. Stitch $\frac{1}{4}$" from each side of drawn lines (Fig. 9). Cut along drawn lines to make 2 Unit 7's. Press seam allowances to light fabrics.

5. Matching corners, place 1 **small square** on each **Unit 7** (Fig. 10).

6. Stitch seam $\frac{1}{4}$" from each side of drawn lines (Fig. 11). Cut along drawn lines to make 4 Flying Geese. Press seam allowances to cream fabric. Flying Geese should measure 2$\frac{1}{2}$" x 4$\frac{1}{2}$" including seam allowances.

7. Repeat Steps 2–6 to make a total of 216 Flying Geese.

8. In color order shown, sew 9 **Flying Geese** (3 pink, 3 blue, and 3 green) together to make Flying Geese Strip. Press seam allowances open or in one direction. Flying Geese Strip should measure 4$\frac{1}{2}$" x 18$\frac{1}{2}$" including seam allowances. Make 24 Flying Geese Strips.

Double Nine Patch Block (make 8)

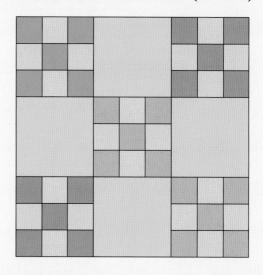

Fig. 8	Fig. 9

Unit 7 (make 2)

Fig. 10	Fig. 11

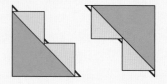

Flying Geese (make 216)

Flying Geese Strip (make 24)

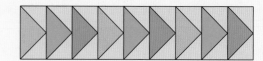

Making the Cornerstones

1. Cut the remaining 32 (16 sets of 2 matching) cream **small squares** *once* diagonally (corner to corner) to make 64 (16 sets of 4 matching) **triangles**.
2. For **Cornerstone**, select 4 matching **triangles** and 1 pink **medium square**.
3. Centering edges and pressing each seam to triangle, sew 2 **triangles** to opposite sides of 1 **medium square**; sew 2 **triangles** to remaining sides to make Cornerstone. Cornerstone should measure $4^1/2$" x $4^1/2$" including seam allowances.
4. Repeat Steps 2–3 to make 16 Cornerstones.

Assembling the Quilt Top Center

1. Making sure geese are pointing in one direction, sew 4 **Cornerstones** and 3 **Flying Geese Strips** together to make Row A. Press seam allowances to Cornerstones. Row A should measure $70^1/2$" x $4^1/2$" including seam allowances. Make 4 Row A's.
2. Sew 4 **Flying Geese Strips** and 3 **Double Nine Patch Blocks** together to make Row B. Press seam allowances to Blocks. Row B should measure $70^1/2$" x $18^1/2$" including seam allowances. Make 2 Row B's.
3. Sew 4 **Flying Geese Strips**, 2 **Double Nine Patch Blocks**, and **House Block** together to make Row C. Press seam allowances to Blocks. Row C should measure $70^1/2$" x $18^1/2$" including seam allowances.
4. Referring to Quilt Top Diagram, page 67, for placement and direction of geese, sew **Rows** together to complete quilt top center. Press seam allowances open or away from Row A's. Quilt top center should measure $70^1/2$" x $70^1/2$" including seam allowances.

Cornerstone (make 16)

Row A (make 4)

Row B (make 2)

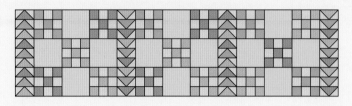

Row C

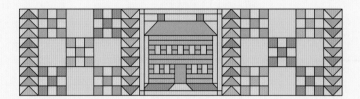

Adding the Border

1. Using diagonal seams (**Fig. 12**), sew 5 **border strips** together to make **border**. Press seam allowances open or in one direction. Make 4 borders.

2. Measure *length* across center of quilt top center. Trim 2 borders to determined measurement for **side borders**. Matching centers and corners, sew side borders to quilt top center.

3. Measure *width* across center of quilt top center (including added borders). Trim remaining borders to determined measurement for **top/bottom borders**. Matching centers and corners, sew top/bottom borders to quilt top.

Fig. 12

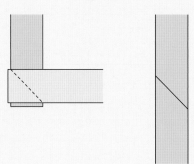

Quilting Detail on House Block

Completing the Quilt

1. Follow **Quilting**, page 108, to mark, layer, and quilt as desired. Quilt shown was machine quilted. A flower was quilted in each large yellow square with green thread. Curved squares were quilted in each square of the nine patches and curved triangles were quilted in the cream portions of the Flying Geese and Cornerstones with blue thread. In the Cornerstones, a flower was quilted in each pink portion and a curved triangle was quilted in each cream portion with blue thread.

A feather pattern was quilted in the border with pink thread. Details were quilted in the House Block, such as blue clouds, green grass, pink roof shingles, blue siding shingles, and yellow curtains.

2. Follow **Making a Hanging Sleeve**, page 109, if a hanging sleeve is desired.

3. Cut a 28" square of binding fabric. Follow **Binding**, page 110, to bind quilt using 2"w bias binding with mitered corners.

Quilt Top Diagram

Jellystone

Quilted by Diane Tricka.

Finished Quilt Size:
74¹/₂" x 74¹/₂"
(189 cm x 189 cm)

Finished Block Size:
13" x 13" (33 cm x 33 cm)

When speaking of Bear Paw quilts, Carrie says she hasn't seen one that she didn't love. Of course, it may have something to do with the use of triangle-squares, which she likes so very much. She does tend to lean toward blocks that use some kind of variation on the traditional Bear Paw. For this quilt, she decided to piece the "paw" part of the block. The name of this quilt? Carrie says, "Yogi Bear lived at Jellystone Park and he wasn't an average bear. Since this isn't the average Bear Paw quilt, 'Jellystone' seemed to fit. Also, I have to admit—I just liked the name."

Yardage Requirements

Yardage is based on 43"/44" (109 cm/112 cm) wide fabric. Fat quarters are approximately 21" x 18" (53 cm x 46 cm).

    8 fat quarters of assorted light print fabrics
    28 fat quarters of assorted dark print fabrics
    $7/8$ yd (80 cm) of fabric for binding
    7 yds (6.4 m)* of fabric for backing
You will also need:
    83" x 83" (211 cm x 211 cm) piece of batting
    Template plastic (optional)

    Yardage is based on 3 lengths of fabric, which allows for a larger backing for long arm quilting. If you are using another quilting method, 2 lengths or $4^5/8$ yds (4.2 m) will be adequate.

Cutting Out the Pieces

*Follow **Rotary Cutting**, page 105, to cut fabric. All measurements include $1/4$" seam allowances.*

From *each* assorted light print fat quarter:

- Cut 3 strips $2^7/8$" x 21". From these strips,
  - Cut 16 **large squares** $2^7/8$" x $2^7/8$". Cut a total of 128 large squares.
- Cut 1 strip $2^1/2$" x 21". From this strip,
  - Cut 8 **small squares** $2^1/2$" x $2^1/2$". Cut a total of 64 small squares.
- Cut 3 strips $1^1/2$" x 21". From these strips,
  - Cut 8 **sashings** $1^1/2$" x $6^1/2$". Cut a total of 64 sashings.

From *each* assorted dark print fat quarter:

- Cut 1 strip $2^7/8$" x 21". From this strip,
  - Cut 5 **large squares** $2^7/8$" x $2^7/8$". Cut a total of 128 large squares.
  - Cut 2 **small squares** $2^1/2$" x $2^1/2$". Cut a total of 56 small squares.
- Cut 2 **wide strips** $2^1/2$" x 21". Cut a total of 51 wide strips.
- Cut 3 **narrow strips** $1^1/2$" x 21". Cut a total of 65 narrow strips.
- Cut 1 strip $5^1/2$" x 21".
  - From *each* of 24 of these $5^1/2$" x 21" strips,
    - Cut 1 **large rectangle** $5^1/2$" x $4^1/2$". Cut a total of 24 large rectangles. *From remainder of strip,*
      - Cut 2 strips $2^1/2$" x $16^1/2$". From these strips,
        - Cut 4 **small rectangles** $2^1/2$" x $3^1/2$". Cut a total of 64 (32 sets of 2 matching) small rectangles.
      - Cut 2 **small squares** $2^1/2$" x $2^1/2$". Cut a total of 33 small squares. You will have 89 small squares.
      - Cut 1 **center square** $1^1/2$" x $1^1/2$". Cut a total of 16 center squares.
  - From *each* of 4 remaining $5^1/2$" x 21" strips,
    - Cut 2 **large rectangles** $5^1/2$" x $4^1/2$". Cut a total of 8 large rectangles. You will have 32 large rectangles.

Making the Triangle-Squares

*Follow **Piecing**, page 106, and **Pressing**, page 107, to assemble the quilt top. Because there are so many seams in this quilt, you may need to use a seam allowance slightly smaller than the usual $1/4$". As you sew, measure your work to compare with the measurements provided and adjust your seam allowance as needed.*

1. Draw a diagonal line (corner to corner) on wrong side of each light **large square**.

2. Matching right sides, place 1 light **large square** on top of 1 dark **large square**. Stitch $1/4$" from each side of drawn line (**Fig. 1**). Cut along drawn line and press seam allowances to dark fabric to make 2 **Triangle-Squares**. Triangle-Square should measure $2^1/2$" x $2^1/2$" including seam allowances. Make a total of 256 Triangle-Squares.

Fig. 1

Triangle-Square (make 256)

Making the Pieced Squares

1. For 2 **Pieced Squares**, select 2 matching dark **small rectangles**, 2 assorted dark **small squares**, and 1 dark **large rectangle**.
2. Sew 1 dark **small square** and 1 dark **small rectangle** together to make **Unit 1**. Press seam allowances to rectangle. Make 2 Unit 1's.
3. Sew 2 **Unit 1's** together to make **Unit 2**. Clip seam allowances as shown in **Fig. 2**, and press seam allowances as indicated by arrows in **Fig. 3**. Unit 2 should measure $4^1/2$" x $5^1/2$" including seam allowances.
4. Draw 2 stitching lines on wrong side of **Unit 2** using either a ruler with a 45° line or templates. Lines should cross the stitching lines at the corner of the squares (**Fig. 4**) and should be slightly over $1/2$" apart. To use ruler, align 45° line on ruler with short edge of **Unit 2** and draw line along long edge of ruler. To make templates, cut a square of template plastic $4^1/2$" x $4^1/2$"; cut square in half diagonally (**Fig. 5**). Align right angle of each template with corner of each square of Unit 2. Draw a line across long edge of each template.
5. Matching right sides, place **Unit 2** on top of **large rectangle**. Stitch across both drawn lines. Cut halfway between drawn lines (**Fig. 6**) and trim seam allowances to $1/4$". Press seam allowances open or to large triangles to make 2 **Pieced Squares**. Pieced Square should measure $4^1/2$" x $4^1/2$" including seam allowances.
6. Repeat Steps 1 – 5 to make a total of 64 Pieced Squares.

Making the Bear Paws

Press seam allowances as indicated by arrows in diagrams.

1. Sew 2 **Triangle-Squares** together to make **Unit 3**. Make 64 Unit 3's.
2. Sew 2 **Triangle-Squares** and 1 light **small square** together to make **Unit 4**. Make 64 Unit 4's.
3. Sew 1 **Unit 3** and 1 **Pieced Square** together to make **Unit 5**. Make 64 Unit 5's.
4. Sew 1 **Unit 4** and 1 **Unit 5** together to make **Bear Paw**. Bear Paw should measure $6^1/2$" x $6^1/2$" including seam allowances. Make 64 Bear Paws.

Unit 1 (make 2)   **Unit 2**

Fig. 2   **Fig. 3**

Fig. 4   **Fig. 5**

Fig. 6

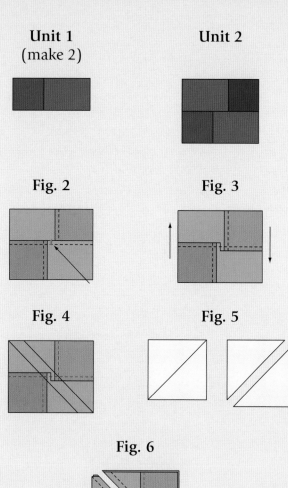

Pieced Square (make 64)

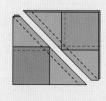

Unit 3 (make 64)   **Unit 4** (make 64)

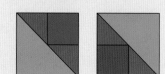

Unit 5 (make 64)   **Bear Paw** (make 64)

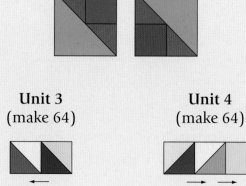

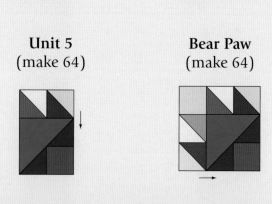

Making the Blocks

1. Sew 2 **Bear Paws** and 1 **sashing** together to make **Unit 6**. Press seam allowances toward sashing. Make 32 Unit 6's.
2. Sew 2 **sashings** and 1 **center square** together to make **Unit 7**. Press seam allowances toward sashings. Make 16 Unit 7's.
3. Sew 2 **Unit 6's** and 1 **Unit 7** together to make **Block**. Press seam allowances to Unit 7. Block should measure $13^1/2$" x $13^1/2$" including seam allowances. Make 16 Blocks.

Making the Pieced Sashings

1. Sew 13 **narrow strips** together to make **Strip Set A**. Press seam allowances in one direction; however, some of these seams may need to be flipped and re-pressed later. Make 5 Strip Set A's. Cut across Strip Set A's at $2^1/2$" intervals to make 40 **pieced sashings**. Pieced sashing should measure $2^1/2$" x $13^1/2$" including seam allowances.

Assembling the Quilt Top Center

1. Sew 4 **pieced sashings** and 5 dark **small squares** together to make **Sashing Row**. Press seam allowances to pieced sashings. Sashing Row should measure $2^1/2$" x $62^1/2$" including seam allowances. Make 5 Sashing Rows.
2. Flipping and re-pressing any seam allowances in pieced sashings as needed, sew 4 **Blocks** and 5 **pieced sashings** together to make **Block Row**. Press seam allowances to pieced sashings. Block Row should measure $13^1/2$" x $62^1/2$" including seam allowances. Make 4 Block Rows.
3. Referring to **Assembly Diagram**, page 74, and flipping and re-pressing any seam allowances in pieced sashings as needed, sew **Rows** together to make quilt top center. Quilt top center should measure $62^1/2$" x $62^1/2$" including seam allowances.

Unit 6 (make 32)

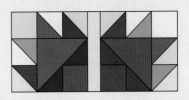

Unit 7 (make 16)

Block (make 16)

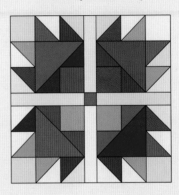

Strip Set A
(make 5)

Pieced Sashing
(make 40)

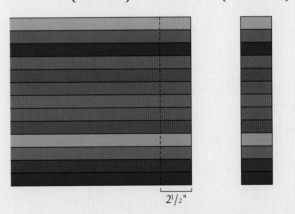

$2^1/2$"

Sashing Row (make 5)

Block Row (make 4)

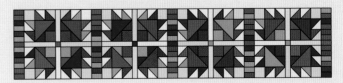

Adding the Border

1. Sew 3 **wide strips** together to make **Strip Set B**. Press seam allowances in one direction. Make 17 Strip Set B's. Cut across Strip Set B's at $2^1/2$" intervals to make 136 **Unit 8's**. Unit 8 should measure $2^1/2$" x $6^1/2$" including seam allowances.

2. Sew 31 **Unit 8's** together to make **side border**. Press seam allowances in one direction. Make 2 side borders. Measure *length* through center of quilt top center. Measure length of side borders. If measurements are not the same, make seams in borders slightly smaller or larger as needed. Matching centers and corners, sew side borders to quilt top center.

3. Sew 37 **Unit 8's** together to make **top border**. Press seam allowances in one direction. Repeat to make **bottom border**. Measure *width* through center of quilt top center (including added borders). Measure length of top/bottom borders. If measurements are not the same, make seams in borders slightly larger or smaller as needed. Matching centers and corners, sew top/bottom borders to quilt top center.

Completing the Quilt

1. To help stabilize the edges and prevent any seams from separating, stay-stitch around the quilt top approximately $1/8$" from the edge.

2. Follow **Quilting**, page 108, to mark, layer, and quilt as desired. Quilt shown was machine quilted. A leaf pattern was quilted in the dark portions of the Bear Paws. The light portions of the Bear Paws were outline quilted and a leaf was quilted in each corner square. A swirl pattern was quilted in the sashings. A feather pattern was quilted in the pieced sashings, with diamonds in the small squares in the Sashing Rows. Swirling diamonds were quilted in the border and outer row of pieced sashings.

3. Follow **Making a Hanging Sleeve**, page 109, if a hanging sleeve is desired.

4. Cut a 27" square of binding fabric. Follow **Binding**, page 110, to bind quilt using 2"w bias binding with mitered corners.

Strip Set B
(make 17)

Unit 8
(make 136)

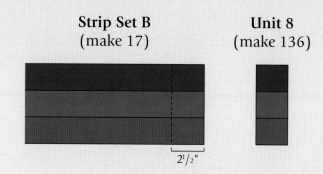

$2^1/2$"

Assembly Diagram

Quilt Top Diagram

Note: This quilt can be made smaller or larger by subtracting or adding Blocks to the length or width. Each Row or Column will change the measurements of the quilt by 15" (13" for the Block and 2" for the sashing).

You may also add more rows of squares to the scrappy border or add a plain border.

Opening Day

Quilted by Diane Tricka.

Finished Quilt Size:
72¹/₂" x 72¹/₂"
(184 cm x 184 cm)

Finished Block Size:
8" x 8" (20 cm x 20 cm)

One of the attractions of quilt design is the way you sometimes get surprised by the way a quilt turns out. Carrie was 200 Flying Geese units into designing this pattern when she realized she already made a quilt very much like the one she had in mind. "While I don't know of any quilters among my ancestors, I do believe my guardian angels were looking out for me," explains Carrie, "because they reminded me I already had all the parts needed to make two of my favorite things, Sawtooth Stars and Flying Geese strips. The funny thing is, this quilt suits the fabric much better than the one I started out to make. My guardian angels must be quilters!" Since the fabric line was named Rites of Spring, Carrie says she was thinking of her favorite springtime event, the return of baseball. Carrie says, with a wink, that it's just a coincidence she finished the quilt on opening day of baseball season.

Yardage Requirements

Yardage is based on 43"/44" (109 cm/112 cm) wide fabric. Fat quarters are approximately 21" x 18" (53 cm x 46 cm).

- 18 fat quarters of assorted light print fabrics
- 18 fat quarters of assorted dark print fabrics
- $^7/_8$ yd (80 cm) of fabric for binding
- $6^3/_4$ yds (6.2 m)* of fabric for backing

You will also need:

- 81" x 81" (206 cm x 206 cm) piece of batting

*Yardage is based on 3 lengths of fabric, which allows for a larger backing for long arm quilting. If you are using another quilting method, 2 lengths or $4^1/_2$ yds (4.1 m), will be adequate.

Cutting Out the Pieces

Follow **Rotary Cutting**, page 105, to cut fabric. All measurements include $^1/_4$" seam allowances.

From *each* light print fat quarter:

- Cut 1 strip $5^1/_4$" x 21". From this strip,
  - Cut 2 **very large squares** $5^1/_4$" x $5^1/_4$". Cut a total of 36 very large squares.
  - Cut 2 **large squares** $4^7/_8$" x $4^7/_8$". Cut a total of 28 large squares.
- Cut 2 strips $2^7/_8$" x 21". From these strips,
  - Cut 8 **small squares** $2^7/_8$" x $2^7/_8$". Cut a total of 128 (32 sets of 4 matching) small squares.
- Cut 2 strips $2^1/_2$" x 21". From these strips,
  - Cut 9 **very small squares** $2^1/_2$" x $2^1/_2$". Cut a total of 160 (36 sets of 4 matching and 16 assorted) very small squares.

From *each* dark print fat quarter:

- Cut 1 strip $5^1/_4$" x 21". From this strip,
  - Cut 2 **very large squares** $5^1/_4$" x $5^1/_4$". Cut a total of 32 very large squares.
  - Cut 2 **large squares** $4^7/_8$" x $4^7/_8$". Cut a total of 28 large squares.
- Cut 2 strips $4^1/_2$" x 21". From these strips,
  - Cut 6 **medium squares** $4^1/_2$" x $4^1/_2$". Cut a total of 92 medium squares.
  - Cut 4 **small squares** $2^7/_8$" x $2^7/_8$". Cut a total of 72 small squares.
- Cut 1 strip $2^7/_8$" x 21". From this strip,
  - Cut 4 **small squares** $2^7/_8$" x $2^7/_8$". Cut a total of 72 small squares. You will have 144 (36 sets of 4 matching) small squares.

Note: Quilt shown includes 36 Sawtooth Star Blocks. Six of these Blocks have Four Patch Centers. You may include as many as you wish. For each Four Patch Center, select 2 dark fabrics of the same color and cut 2 **very small squares** $2^1/_2$" x $2^1/_2$" from each fabric.

Making the Flying Geese

Follow **Piecing**, page 106, and **Pressing**, page 107, to assemble the quilt top. Because there are so many seams in this quilt, you may need to use a seam allowance slightly smaller than the usual $1/4$". As you sew, measure your work to compare with the measurements provided and adjust your seam allowance as needed.

1. Draw a diagonal line (corner to corner) on wrong side of each dark print **small square** and each light print **small square**.

2. For 4 matching **Flying Geese A's**, select 4 matching dark **small squares** and 1 light **very large square**.

3. Matching right sides, place 1 **small square** on opposite corners of **very large square** (**Fig. 1**); pin in place.

Fig. 1

4. Stitch ¹/₄" from each side of drawn lines (**Fig. 2**). Cut along drawn lines to make 2 **Unit 1**'s. Press seam allowances to dark fabric.
5. Matching corners, place 1 **small square** on each **Unit 1** (**Fig. 3**). 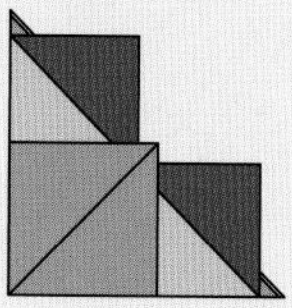
6. Stitch seam ¹/₄" from each side of drawn lines (**Fig. 4**). Cut along drawn lines to make 4 matching **Flying Geese A's**. Press seam allowances to dark fabric. Flying Geese should measure 2¹/₂" x 4¹/₂" including seam allowances.
7. Repeat Steps 2–6 to make 36 sets of 4 matching Flying Geese A's.
8. Using light **small squares** and dark **very large squares** and pressing seam allowances to light fabric, repeat Steps 2–6 to make 128 **Flying Geese B's**.

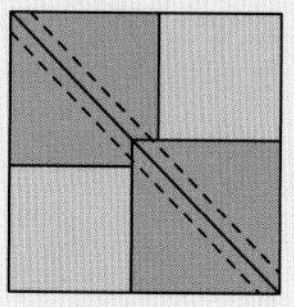

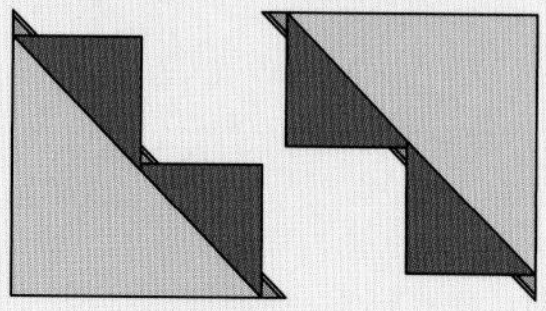

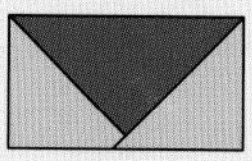

Making the Triangle-Squares

1. Draw a diagonal line (corner to corner) on wrong side each light **large square**.
2. Matching right sides, place 1 light **large square** on top of 1 dark **large square**. Stitch ¹/₄" from each side of drawn line (**Fig. 5**). Cut along drawn line and press seam allowances to dark fabric to make 2 **Triangle-Squares**. Triangle-Square should measure 4¹/₂" x 4¹/₂" including seam allowances. Make 56 Triangle-Squares.

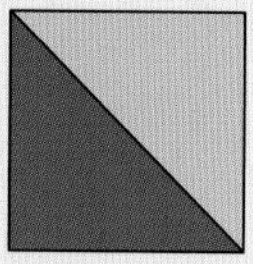

Making the Sawtooth Star Blocks

1. For **Sawtooth Star Block**, select 4 matching **Flying Geese A's** and 4 light **very small squares** of the same light fabric as in the Flying Geese. For center, select 1 dark **medium square** of the same dark fabric as in the Flying Geese *OR* if you are including Four Patches, select the 4 **very small squares** cut for 1 **Four Patch Center**.
2. Sew 1 **Flying Geese A** and 2 **very small squares** together to make **Unit 2**. Press seam allowances open or to very small squares. Make 2 Unit 2's.
*If not making **Four Patch Center**, skip to Step 5.*
3. Sew 2 different dark print **very small squares** together to make **Unit 3**. Press seam allowances open or to one side. Make 2 Unit 3's.

Fig. 2

Unit 1 (make 2)

Fig. 3   **Fig. 4**

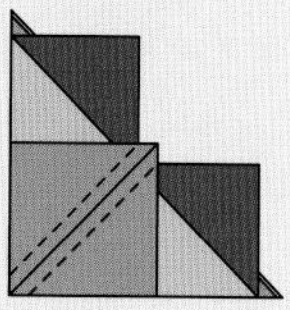

Flying Geese A
(make 36 sets of 4 matching)

Flying Geese B (make 128)

Fig. 5

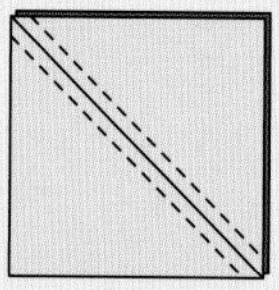

Triangle-Square (make 56)

Unit 2 (make 2)

Unit 3 (make 2)

4. Sew 2 **Unit 3's** together to make **Four Patch Center**. To press seam allowances, follow **Collapsing the Seams**, page 107. Four Patch Center should measure 4¹/₂" x 4¹/₂" including seam allowances.
5. Sew 2 **Flying Geese** and **medium square** *OR* **Four Patch Center** together to make **Unit 4**. Press seam allowances open or to the center.
6. Sew 2 **Unit 2's** and **Unit 4** together to make **Sawtooth Star Block**. Press seam allowances open or to Unit 4. Sawtooth Star Block should measure 8¹/₂" x 8¹/₂" including seam allowances.
7. Repeat Steps 1–6 to make 36 Sawtooth Star Blocks.

Making the Cotton Reel Blocks
1. For each **Cotton Reel Block**, select 2 assorted dark **medium squares** and 2 assorted **Triangle-Squares**.
2. Sew 1 **medium square** and 1 **Triangle-Square** together to make **Unit 5**. Press seam allowances open or to medium square. Make 2 Unit 5's.
3. Sew 2 **Unit 5's** together to make **Cotton Reel Block**. To press seam allowances, follow **Collapsing the Seams**, page 107. Cotton Reel Block should measure 8¹/₂" x 8¹/₂" including seam allowances.
4. Repeat Steps 1–3 to make 28 Cotton Reel Blocks.

Assembling the Quilt Top Center
1. Sew 6 **Sawtooth Star Blocks** together to make **Row**. Make 6 Rows. Press seam allowances open or press them in one direction in every other Row and in the opposite direction in remaining Rows. Row should measure 8¹/₂" x 48¹/₂" including seam allowances.
2. Referring to **Quilt Top Diagram**, page 83, sew **Rows** together to make quilt top center. Press seam allowances open or in one direction. Quilt top center should measure 48¹/₂" x 48¹/₂" including seam allowances.

Making the Flying Geese Strips
1. Sew 24 **Flying Geese B's** together to make **Unit 6**. Press seam allowances open or in one direction. Unit 6 should measure 4¹/₂" x 48¹/₂" including seam allowances. Make 4 Unit 6's.

Four Patch Center

Unit 4

 *or*

Sawtooth Star Block (make 36)

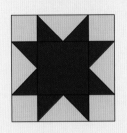 *or*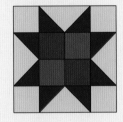

Unit 5 (make 2)   Cotton Reel Block (make 28)

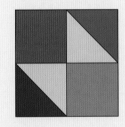

Row (make 6)

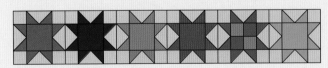

Unit 6 (make 4)

2. Sew 4 **Flying Geese B's** together to make
Unit 7. Press seam allowances open or in one
direction. Unit 7 should measure 4^1/$_2$" x 8^1/$_2$"
including seam allowances. Make 8 Unit 7's.

Making the Four Patch Cornerstones

1. Sew 2 assorted light **very small squares**
together to make Unit 8. Press seam
allowances to one side. Make 2 Unit 8's.
2. Sew 2 **Unit 8's** together to make Four Patch
Cornerstone. To press seam allowances, refer
to **Collapsing the Seams**, page 107. Four
Patch Cornerstone should measure 4^1/$_2$" x 4^1/$_2$"
including seam allowances.
3. Repeat Steps 1–2 to make 4 Four Patch
Cornerstones.

Assembling the Side Sections

1. Sew 6 **Cotton Reel Blocks** together to make
Unit 9. Press seam allowances open or in one
direction. **Unit 9** should measure 8^1/$_2$" x 48^1/$_2$"
including seam allowances. Make 2 **Unit 9's**.
2. Sew 1 **Unit 6** and 1 **Unit 9** together to make
Side Section. Press seam allowances open or
to Unit 9. Side Section should measure
12^1/$_2$" x 48^1/$_2$" including seam allowances.
Make 2 Side Sections.

Assembling the Top and Bottom Sections

1. Sew 8 **Cotton Reel Blocks** and 2 **Unit 7's**
together to make Unit 10. Press seam
allowances open or away from the Unit 7's.
Unit 10 should measure 8^1/$_2$" x 72^1/$_2$" including
seam allowances. Make 2 Unit 10's.
2. Sew 1 **Unit 6**, 2 **Unit 7's**, and 2 **Four Patch
Cornerstones** together to make Unit 11. Press
seam allowances open or to the Four Patch
Cornerstones. Unit 11 should measure
4^1/$_2$" x 72^1/$_2$" including seam allowances.
Make 2 Unit 11's.
3. Sew 1 **Unit 10** and 1 **Unit 11** together to make
Top Section. Press seam allowances open or to
Unit 10. Top Section should measure
12^1/$_2$" x 72^1/$_2$" including seam allowances.
Repeat to make Bottom Section.

Unit 7 (make 8)

Unit 8
(make 2)

Four Patch Cornerstone
(make 4)

Unit 9 (make 2)

Side Section (make 2)

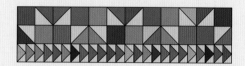

Unit 10 (make 2)

Unit 11 (make 2)

Top/Bottom Section (make 2)

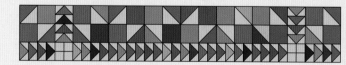

Assembling the Quilt Top

Refer to Quilt Top Diagram for placement.

1. Sew **Side Sections** to opposite sides of quilt top center. Press seam allowances open or to quilt top center. Quilt top center/Side Sections should measure $72^1/2$" x $48^1/2$" including seam allowances.
2. Sew **Top** and **Bottom Sections** to quilt top center/Side Sections to complete quilt top. Press seam allowances open or to Top/Bottom Sections. Quilt top should measure $72^1/2$" x $72^1/2$" including seam allowances.

Completing the Quilt

1. To help stabilize the edges and prevent any seams from separating, stay-stitch around the quilt top approximately $1/8$" from the edge.

2. Follow **Quilting**, page 108, to mark, layer, and quilt as desired. Quilt shown was machine quilted. In the ditch quilting was quilted around the Sawtooth Star Blocks and the Flying Geese units. The Sawtooth Star Blocks were quilted with swirling patterns in the stars, triangles in the corners (making diamond shapes with the adjacent blocks), and loops in the Flying Geese. Feather patterns were quilting in the Flying Geese units and Cotton Reel Blocks. The diamond shapes were repeated in the Four Patch Cornerstones.

3. Follow **Making a Hanging Sleeve**, page 109, if a hanging sleeve is desired.

4. Cut a 27" square of binding fabric. Follow **Binding**, page 110, to bind quilt using 2"w bias binding with mitered corners.

Quilt Top Diagram

Note: To make quilt smaller or larger, subtract or add a Row or Column of Sawtooth Star Blocks to the quilt top center. This will change the dimension of the quilt by 8". You will need to subtract or add 8 Flying Geese and 2 Cotton Reel Blocks for each Row or Column.

Raise the Roof

Quilted by Diane Tricka.

Finished Quilt Size:
74¹/₂" x 74¹/₂"
(189 cm x 189 cm)

Finished Block Size:
8" x 8" (20 cm x 20 cm)

Carrie started designing this quilt with an ultimate goal in mind—working stars into a Log Cabin quilt without using sashing or putting the stars in the center of the Log Cabins. She says she just started drawing lines until she arrived at this pattern. There are 32 blocks each of Log Cabin and Sawtooth Star. Carrie's use of triangle-squares and the assortment of fabric prints are what make the unique handling of light and dark possible. The quilt uses a Barn Raising setting for the Log Cabin Blocks, but with the addition of stars, Carrie thought "Raise the Roof" perfectly captured the spirit of this heavenly creation.

Yardage Requirements

Yardage is based on 43"/44" (109 cm/112 cm) wide fabric. Fat quarters are approximately 21" x 18" (53 cm x 46 cm).

13 fat quarters of assorted light prints
19 fat quarters of assorted dark prints
7/8 yd (80 cm) of fabric for binding
7 yds (6.4 m)* of fabric for backing

You will also need:

83" x 83" (211 cm x 211 cm) piece of batting

*Yardage is based on 3 lengths of fabric, which allows for a larger backing for long arm quilting. If you are using another quilting method, 2 lengths or $4^5/8$ yds (4.2 m), will be adequate.

Cutting Out the Pieces

*Follow **Rotary Cutting**, page 105, to cut fabric. All measurements include 1/4" seam allowances.*

From *each* of 9 assorted light print fat quarter:

- Cut 1 strip $5^1/4$" x 21". From this strip,
  - Cut 2 **large squares** $5^1/4$" x $5^1/4$". Cut a total of 18 large squares.
  - *From remainder of strip,*
    - Cut 1 strip $2^7/8$" x $10^1/2$". From this strip,
      - Cut 3 **medium squares** $2^7/8$" x $2^7/8$". Cut a total of 27 medium squares.
    - Cut 1 **strip** $1^1/2$" x $10^1/2$". Cut a total of 9 strips. *Set aside.*
  - Cut 1 strip $2^7/8$" x 21". From this strip,
    - Cut 5 **medium squares** $2^7/8$" x $2^7/8$". Cut a total of 45 medium squares.
    - Cut 2 **small squares** $2^1/2$" x $2^1/2$". Cut a total of 18 small squares.
  - Cut 6 **strips** $1^1/2$" x 21". Cut a total of 54 strips. *Set aside.*

From *each* of remaining 4 assorted light print fat quarter:

- Cut 1 strip $5^1/4$" x 21". From this strip,
  - Cut 4 **large squares** $5^1/4$" x $5^1/4$". Cut a total of 14 large squares. You will have 32 large squares.
  - Cut 2 strips $2^7/8$" x 21". From these strips,
    - Cut 10 **medium squares** $2^7/8$" x $2^7/8$". Cut a total of 40 medium squares. You will have 112 medium squares.

- Cut 4 **small squares** $2^1/2$" x $2^1/2$". Cut a total of 14 small squares. You will have 32 small squares.
- Cut 3 **strips** $1^1/2$" x 21". Cut a total of 9 strips. *Set aside.* You will have 63 long (21") strips.

From *each* of 16 assorted dark print fat quarter:

- Cut 1 strip $5^1/4$" x 21". From this strip,
  - Cut 2 **large squares** $5^1/4$" x $5^1/4$". Cut a total of 32 large squares.
  - *From remainder of strip,*
    - Cut 1 strip $2^7/8$" x $10^1/2$". From this strip,
      - Cut 3 **medium squares** $2^7/8$" x $2^7/8$". Cut a total of 48 medium squares.
    - Cut 1 **strip** $1^1/2$" x $10^1/2$". Cut a total of 16 strips. *Set aside.*
- Cut 1 strip $2^7/8$" x 21". From this strip,
  - Cut 4 **medium squares** $2^7/8$" x $2^7/8$". Cut a total of 64 medium squares. You will have 112 medium squares.
  - Cut 2 **small squares** $2^1/2$" x $2^1/2$". Cut a total of 32 small squares.
- Cut 6 **strips** $1^1/2$" x 21". Cut a total of 96 strips. *Set aside.*

From *each* of remaining 3 assorted dark print fat quarters:

- Cut 9 **strips** $1^1/2$" x 21". Cut a total of 26 strips. *Set aside.* You will have 122 long (21") strips.

From light strips set aside:

- Select 15 long (21") **strips** for the inner border. *Set aside.*
- From *each* of 9 short ($10^1/2$") **strips**,
  - Cut 4 **rectangle #1's** $1^1/2$" x $2^1/2$". Cut a total of 32 rectangle #1's.
- From *each* of 16 long (21") **strips**,
  - Cut 2 **rectangle #2's** $1^1/2$" x $3^1/2$". Cut a total of 32 rectangle #2's.
  - Cut 2 **rectangle #5's** $1^1/2$" x $4^1/2$". Cut a total of 32 rectangle #5's.
- From *each* of 32 long (21") **strips**,
  - Cut 1 **rectangle #6** $1^1/2$" x $5^1/2$". Cut a total of 32 rectangle #6's.
  - Cut 1 **rectangle #9** $1^1/2$" x $6^1/2$". Cut a total of 32 rectangle #9's.
  - Cut 1 **rectangle #10** $1^1/2$" x $7^1/2$". Cut a total of 32 rectangle #10's.

From dark strips set aside:

- Select 66 long (21") **strips** for the outer border. *Set aside.*
- From *each* of 16 short (10½") **strips,**
  - Cut 1 **rectangle #12** 1½" x 8½". Cut a total of 16 rectangle #12's.
- From *each* of 32 long (21") **strips,**
  - Cut 1 **rectangle #3** 1½" x 3½". Cut a total of 32 rectangle #3's.
  - Cut 1 **rectangle #4** 1½" x 4½". Cut a total of 32 rectangle #4's.
  - Cut 1 **rectangle #7** 1½" x 5½". Cut a total of 32 rectangle #7's.
  - Cut 1 **rectangle #8** 1½" x 6½". Cut a total of 32 rectangle #8's.

- From *each* of 16 long (21") **strips,**
  - Cut 1 **rectangle #11** 1½" x 7½". Cut a total of 16 rectangle #11's.
  - Cut 1 **rectangle #12** 1½" x 8½". Cut a total of 16 rectangle #12's. You will have 32 rectangle #12's.
- From *each* of 8 long (21") **strips,**
  - Cut 2 **rectangle #11's** 1½" x 7½". Cut a total of 16 rectangle #11's. You will have 32 rectangle #11's.
- From left over pieces of dark strips, cut a total of 32 **corner rectangles** 1½" x 2½".

Making the Flying Geese

Follow **Piecing**, page 106, and **Pressing**, page 107, to assemble the quilt top. Because there are so many seams in this quilt, you may need to use a seam allowance slightly smaller than the usual ¹/₄". As you sew, measure your work to compare with the measurements provided and adjust your seam allowance as needed.

1. Draw a diagonal line (corner to corner) across 64 light **medium squares** and 64 dark **medium squares**.

2. For 4 **Dark Flying Geese**, select 4 assorted marked light **medium squares** and 1 dark **large square**.

3. Matching right sides, place 1 **medium square** on opposite corners of **large square** (**Fig. 1**); pin in place.

4. Stitch ¹/₄" from each side of drawn lines (**Fig. 2**). Cut along drawn lines to make 2 **Unit 1's**. Press seam allowances to light fabrics.

5. Matching corners, place 1 **medium square** on each **Unit 1** (**Fig. 3**).

6. Stitch seam ¹/₄" from each side of drawn lines (**Fig. 4**). Cut along drawn lines to make 4 **Dark Flying Geese**. Press seam allowances to light fabric. Dark Flying Geese should measure 2¹/₂" x 4¹/₂" including seam allowances.

7. Repeat Steps 2–6 to make a total of 64 Dark Flying Geese.

8. Using dark **medium squares** and light **large squares** and pressing seam allowances to dark fabrics, repeat Steps 3–6 to make 64 **Light Flying Geese**. Light Flying Geese should measure 2¹/₂" x 4¹/₂" including seam allowances.

Making the Triangle-Squares

1. Draw a diagonal line (corner to corner) on wrong side of each remaining light **medium square**.

2. Matching right sides, place 1 light **medium square** on top of 1 dark **medium square**. Stitch ¹/₄" from each side of drawn line (**Fig. 5**). Cut along drawn line and press seam allowances to dark fabric to make 2 **Triangle-Squares**. Triangle-Square should measure 2¹/₂" x 2¹/₂" including seam allowances. Make a total of 96 Triangle-Squares.

Fig. 1

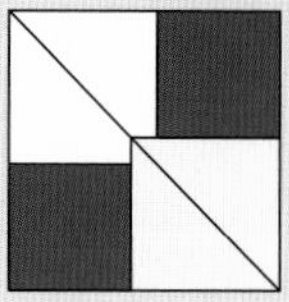

Fig. 2

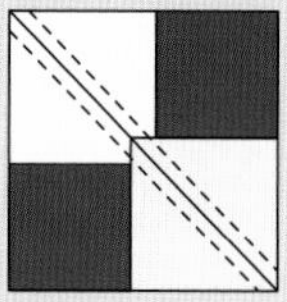

Unit 1 (make 2)

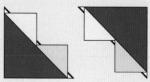

Fig. 3

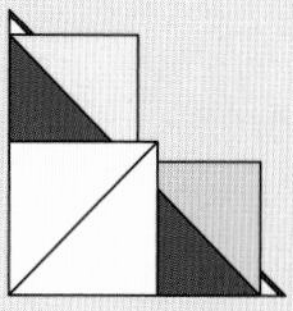

Fig. 4

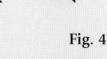

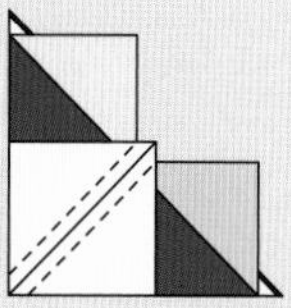

Dark Flying Geese (make 64)

Light Flying Geese (make 64)

Fig. 5

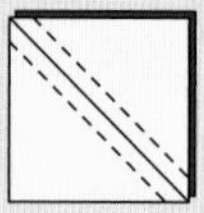

Triangle-Square (make 96)

Making the Hourglasses

1. Draw a diagonal line (corner to corner) on wrong side of 8 light **large squares** and 8 dark **large squares**.

2. Matching right sides, place 1 marked light **large square** on top of 1 unmarked light **large square**. Stitch $1/4$" from each side of drawn line. Cut along drawn line and press seam allowances to one side to make 2 **Light Triangle-Squares**. Light Triangle-Square should measure $4^7/8$" x $4^7/8$" including seam allowances. Make a total of 16 Light Triangle-Squares.

3. Use dark **large squares** to make a total of 16 **Dark Triangle-Squares**. Dark Triangle-Square should measure $4^7/8$" x $4^7/8$" including seam allowances.

4. On wrong side of each **Light Triangle-Square**, draw a diagonal line (corner to corner and perpendicular to seam).

5. Matching right sides and seams, place 1 **Light Triangle-Square** on top of 1 **Dark Triangle-Square**. Stitch $1/4$" from each side of drawn line (**Fig. 6**). Cut apart along drawn line to make 2 **Hourglasses** and press seam allowances to dark fabric. Hourglass should measure $4^1/2$" x $4^1/2$" including seam allowances. Make a total of 32 Hourglasses.

Making the Sawtooth Star Blocks

1. Sew 1 light **small square**, 1 **Light Flying Geese**, and 1 **Triangle-Square** together to make **Unit 2**. Press seam allowances away from Flying Geese.

2. Sew 1 **Light Flying Geese**, 1 **Hourglass**, and 1 **Dark Flying Geese** together to make **Unit 3**. Press seam allowances away from Flying Geese.

3. Sew 1 **Triangle-Square**, 1 **Dark Flying Geese**, and 1 dark **small square** together to make **Unit 4**. Press seam allowances away from Flying Geese.

4. Sew **Unit 2**, **Unit 3**, and **Unit 4** together to make **Sawtooth Star Block**. Press seam allowances open or to Unit 3. Sawtooth Star Block should measure $8^1/2$" x $8^1/2$" including seam allowances.

5. Repeat Steps 1–4 to make a total of 32 Sawtooth Star Blocks.

Light Triangle-Square (make 16)

Dark Triangle-Square (make 16)

Fig. 6

Hourglass (make 32)

Unit 2   **Unit 3**

Unit 4

Sawtooth Star Block (make 32)

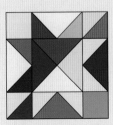

Making the Log Cabin Blocks

1. Sew 1 **Triangle-Square** and 1 **rectangle #1** together to make **Unit 5**. Press seam allowances to rectangle #1.
2. Sew **Unit 5** and 1 **rectangle #2** together to make **Unit 6**. Press seam allowances to rectangle #2.
3. Sew **Unit 6** and 1 **rectangle #3** together to make **Unit 7**. Press seam allowances to rectangle #3.
4. Sew **Unit 7** and 1 **rectangle #4** together to make **Unit 8**. Press seam allowances to rectangle #4.
5. In the same manner, add **rectangles #5–#12** in numerical order to make **Log Cabin Block**, rotating Block and pressing each seam to last rectangle added. Log Cabin Block should measure $8^1/_2$" x $8^1/_2$" including seam allowances.
6. Repeat Steps 1–5 to make a total of 32 Log Cabin Blocks.

Assembling the Quilt Top Center

1. Referring to **Quilt Top Diagram**, arrange **Blocks** into 8 **Rows** of 8 Blocks. Pay attention to the placement of the light and dark halves of the Blocks.
2. Sew 8 **Blocks** together to make **Row**. Make 8 Rows. Press seam allowances open or press them in one direction in every other Row and in the opposite direction in remaining Rows.
3. Sew **Rows** together to make quilt top center. Press seam allowances open or in one direction. Quilt top center should measure $64^1/_2$" x $64^1/_2$" including seam allowances.

Adding the Inner Border

1. Using diagonal seams (**Fig. 7**), sew light **strips** selected for inner border together into a continuous strip approximately $7^3/_4$ yds long.
2. To determine length of **side inner borders**, measure *length* across center of quilt top center. Cut 2 side inner borders from continuous strip. Matching centers and corners, sew side inner borders to quilt top center.
3. To determine length of **top/bottom inner borders**, measure *width* across center of quilt top center (including added borders). Cut 2 top/bottom inner borders from continuous strip. Matching centers and corners, sew top/bottom inner borders to quilt top center.

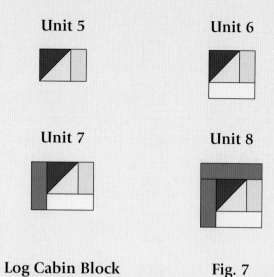

Unit 5 Unit 6

Unit 7 Unit 8

Log Cabin Block (make 32) Fig. 7

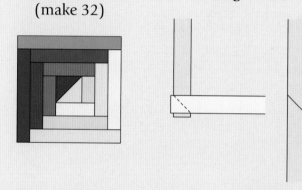

Strip Set (make 6) **Unit 9** (make 24)

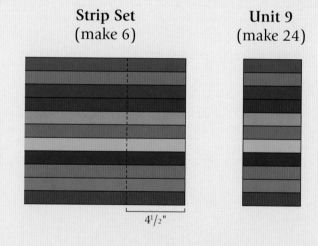

$4^1/_2$"

Outer Border (make 4)

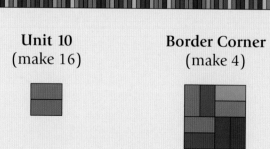

Unit 10 (make 16) **Border Corner** (make 4)

Adding the Outer Border

1. Sew 11 dark **strips** selected for outer border together to make **Strip Set**. Make 6 **Strip Sets**. Cut across **Strip Sets** at $4^1/_2$" intervals to make 24 **Unit 9's**.

2. Sew 6 **Unit 9's** together to make **outer border**. Make 4 outer borders.

3. Sew 2 **corner rectangles** together to make **Unit 10**. Make 16 Unit 10's.

4. Sew 4 **Unit 10's** together to make **border corner**. Border corner should measure $4^1/_2$" x $4^1/_2$". Make 4 border corners.

5. Measure *length* across center of quilt top. Measure length of 2 outer borders for **side outer borders**. If measurements are not the same, make some of the seams in borders slightly larger or smaller as needed. Matching centers and corners, sew side outer borders to quilt top.

6. Sew 1 **border corner** to each end of each remaining outer border to make **top/bottom outer borders**. Measure *width* across center of quilt top (including added borders). Measure length of top/bottom outer borders. If measurements are not the same, make some of the seams in borders slightly larger or smaller as needed. Matching centers and corners, sew top/bottom outer borders to quilt top. Quilt top should measure $74^1/_2$" x $74^1/_2$" including seam allowances.

Completing the Quilt

1. To help stabilize the edges and prevent any seams from separating, stay-stitch around the quilt top approximately $^1/_8$" from the edge.

2. Follow **Quilting**, page 108, to mark, layer, and quilt as desired. Quilt shown was machine quilted with maroon thread in the dark areas and cream thread in the light areas. The inner border and border corners were stitched in the ditch. A feather pattern was quilted through the inner border and dark areas of the Blocks. A flower pattern with straight lines and a leaf pattern were quilted in the light areas of the Blocks. A loop pattern was quilted in the outer border.

3. Follow **Making a Hanging Sleeve**, page 109, if a hanging sleeve is desired.

4. Cut a 27" square of binding fabric. Follow **Binding**, page 110, to bind quilt using 2"w bias binding with mitered corners.

Quilt Top Diagram

True Blue

Quilted by Diane Tricka.

Finished Quilt Size:
80¹/₂" x 80¹/₂"
(204 cm x 204 cm)

Finished Block Size:
7" x 7" (18 cm x 18 cm)

"There is nothing better in this world than a 'true blue friend,'" says Carrie, "especially if that friend is also a quilter. After that, everything else is a distant second—except maybe for chocolate." When it comes to quilts, Carrie feels that any design that is relatively easy to make and works in any fabric style or color palette qualifies as a "true blue quilt-friend." As Carrie says, "Just as we choose our friends, we can choose our fabric-friends with this quilt." You can use lights and darks in two color groups for the blocks of this design. Or you can use a large assortment of colors and fabrics and make blocks where the only thing you worry about is that one fabric is lighter than the other.

Yardage Requirements

Yardage is based on 43"/44" (109 cm/112 cm) wide fabric. Fat quarters are approximately 21" x 18" (53 cm x 46 cm).

16 fat quarters of assorted tan prints
22 fat quarters of assorted blue prints
$7/8$ yd (80 cm) of fabric for binding
$7^1/2$ yds (6.9 m) of fabric for backing

You will also need:

89" x 89" (226 cm x 226 cm) piece of batting

Cutting Out the Pieces

*Follow **Rotary Cutting**, page 105, to cut fabric. All measurements include $1/4$" seam allowances.*

From *each* of 13 assorted tan print fat quarters:

- Cut 1 strip $4^7/8$" x 21". From this strip,
  - Cut 3 **large squares** $4^7/8$" x $4^7/8$". Cut a total of 39 large squares.
  - Cut 2 **small rectangles** 2" x $4^1/2$". Cut a total of 26 small rectangles.
- Cut 1 strip $2^3/8$" x 21". From this strip,
  - Cut 6 **small squares** $2^3/8$" x $2^3/8$". Cut a total of 78 small squares.
- Cut 2 strips 2" x 21". From these strips,
  - Cut 6 **large rectangles** 2" x 6". Cut a total of 78 large rectangles.
- Cut 1 strip 2" x 21". From this strip,
  - Cut 4 **small rectangles** 2" x $4^1/2$". Cut a total of 52 small rectangles.
- Cut 2 **inner border strips** $1^1/2$" x 21". Cut a total of 16 inner border strips.

From *each* of remaining 3 assorted tan print fat quarters:

- Cut 1 strip $4^7/8$" x 21". From this strip,
  - Cut 4 **large squares** $4^7/8$" x $4^7/8$". Cut a total of 12 large squares. You will have 51 large squares.
- Cut 1 strip $2^3/8$" x 21". From this strip,
  - Cut 8 **small squares** $2^3/8$" x $2^3/8$". Cut a total of 24 small squares. You will have 102 small squares.
- Cut 5 strips 2" x 21". From these strips,
  - Cut 8 **large rectangles** 2" x 6". Cut a total of 24 large rectangles. You will have 102 large rectangles.
  - Cut 8 **small rectangles** 2" x $4^1/2$". Cut a total of 24 small rectangles. You will have 102 small rectangles.

From *each* of 12 assorted blue print fat quarter:

- Cut 1 strip $4^7/8$" x 21". From this strip,
  - Cut 2 **large squares** $4^7/8$" x $4^7/8$". Cut a total of 24 large squares.

From remainder of strip,

- Cut 1 strip $2^3/8$" x $11^1/4$". From this strip, cut 4 **small squares** $2^3/8$" x $2^3/8$". Cut a total of 48 small squares.
- Cut 3 strips 2" x 21". From these strips,
  - Cut 4 **large rectangles** 2" x 6". Cut a total of 48 large rectangles.
  - Cut 4 **small rectangles** 2" x $4^1/2$". Cut a total of 48 small rectangles.
- Cut 3 **outer border strips** 2" x 21". Cut a total of 36 outer border strips.

From *each* of remaining 10 assorted blue print fat quarters:

- Cut 1 strip $4^7/8$" x 21". From this strip,
  - Cut 3 **large squares** $4^7/8$" x $4^7/8$". Cut a total of 30 large squares. You will have 54 large squares.
  - Cut 2 **small rectangles** 2" x $4^1/2$". Cut a total of 20 small rectangles.
- Cut 1 strip $2^3/8$" x 21". From this strip,
  - Cut 6 **small squares** $2^3/8$" x $2^3/8$". Cut a total of 60 small squares. You will have 108 small squares.
- Cut 3 strips 2" x 21". From these strips,
  - Cut 6 **large rectangles** 2" x 6". Cut a total of 60 large rectangles. You will have 108 large rectangles.
  - Cut 4 **small rectangles** 2" x $4^1/2$". Cut a total of 40 small rectangles. You will have 108 small rectangles.
- Cut 2 **outer border strips** 2" x 21". Cut a total of 12 outer border strips. You will have 48 outer border strips.

Making Blocks

Follow **Piecing**, page 106, and **Pressing**, page 107, to assemble the quilt top. Because there are so many seams in this quilt, you may need to use a seam allowance slightly smaller than the usual ¹/₄". As you sew, measure your work to compare with the measurements provided and adjust your seam allowance as needed.

1. To make 2 **Blocks**, select 1 **large square**, 2 **small squares**, 2 **large rectangles**, and 2 **small rectangles** of 1 tan print. Also, select 1 **large square**, 2 **small squares**, 2 **large rectangles**, and 2 **small rectangles** of 1 blue print.

2. Draw a diagonal line (corner to corner) on wrong side of each tan **large square** and each tan **small square**.

3. Matching right sides, place 1 tan **small square** on top of 1 blue **small square**. Stitch ¹/₄" from each side of drawn line (**Fig. 1**). Cut along drawn line and press seam allowances to blue fabric to make 2 **Small Triangle-Squares**. Small Triangle-Square should measure 2" x 2" including seam allowances. Make 4 Small Triangle-Squares.

Fig. 1

Small Triangle-Square
(make 4)

true blue 95

4. Use tan **large square** and blue **large square** to make 2 **Large Triangle-Squares**. Large Triangle-Square should measure $4^{1}/_{2}$" x $4^{1}/_{2}$" including seam allowances.

5. Sew 1 **Large Triangle-Square** and 1 tan **small rectangle** together to make **Unit 1**. Press seam allowances to small rectangle. Make 2 Unit 1's.

6. Sew 1 **Unit 1** and 1 tan **large rectangle** together to make **Unit 2**. Press seam allowances to large rectangle. Make 2 Unit 2's.

7. Sew 1 **Small Triangle-Square** and 1 blue **small rectangle** together to make **Unit 3**. Press seam allowances to small rectangle. Make 2 Unit 3's.

8. Sew 1 **Unit 2** and 1 **Unit 3** together to make **Unit 4**. Press seam allowances to Unit 3. Make 2 Unit 4's.

9. Sew 1 **Small Triangle-Square** and 1 blue **large rectangle** together to make **Unit 5**. Press seam allowances to large rectangle. Make 2 Unit 5's.

10. Sew 1 **Unit 4** and 1 **Unit 5** together to make **Block**. Press seam allowances to Unit 5. Block should measure $7^{1}/_{2}$" x $7^{1}/_{2}$" including seam allowances. Make 2 Blocks.

11. Repeat Steps 1–10 to make 100 Blocks. *(Note: Set aside remaining 4 blue **large squares** for outer border.)*

Assembling the Quilt Top Center

1. Referring to **Quilt Top Diagram**, sew 10 **Blocks** together to make **Row**. Press seam allowances open or press them in one direction in every other Row and in the opposite direction in remaining Rows. Make 10 Rows.

2. Sew **Rows** together to complete quilt top center. Press seam allowances open or in one direction. Quilt top center should measure $70^{1}/_{2}$" x $70^{1}/_{2}$" including seam allowances.

Adding the Inner Border

1. Using diagonal seams (**Fig. 2**), sew tan **inner border strips** together into a continuous strip approximately $8^{1}/_{2}$ yds long. Press seam allowances open.

2. To determine length of **side inner borders**, measure *length* across center of quilt top center. Cut 2 side inner borders from continuous strip. Matching centers and corners, sew side inner borders to quilt top center.

3. To determine length of **top/bottom inner borders**, measure *width* across center of quilt top center. Cut 2 top/bottom inner borders from continuous strip. Matching centers and corners, sew top/bottom inner borders to quilt top center.

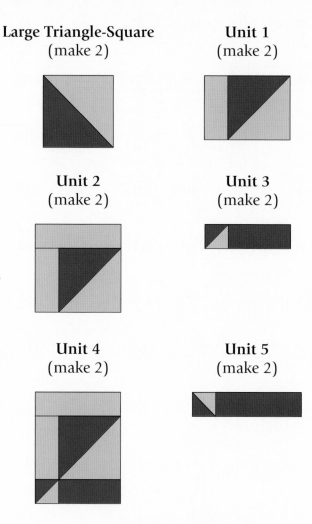

Large Triangle-Square (make 2)

Unit 1 (make 2)

Unit 2 (make 2)

Unit 3 (make 2)

Unit 4 (make 2)

Unit 5 (make 2)

Block (make 100)

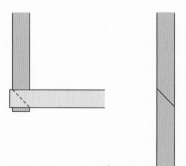

Fig. 2

Adding the Outer Border

1. Sew 8 blue **outer border strips** together to make **Strip Set**. Make 6 Strip Sets. Cut across Strip Sets at 4¹/₂" intervals to make 24 **Unit 6's**. Unit 6 should measure 4¹/₂" x 12¹/₂" including seam allowances.

2. Sew 6 **Unit 6's** together to make **outer border**. Press seam allowances in one direction or open. Make 4 outer borders.

3. Draw a diagonal line (corner to corner) on wrong side of 2 remaining blue **large squares**.

4. Matching right sides, place 1 marked blue **large square** on top of 1 unmarked blue **large square**. Stitch ¹/₄" from each side of drawn line (**Fig. 3**). Cut along drawn line and press seam allowances in one direction to make 2 **Border Triangle-Squares**. Border Triangle-Square should measure 4¹/₂" x 4¹/₂" including seam allowances. Make 4 Border Triangle-Squares.

5. Measure *length* across center of quilt top. Measure length of 2 outer borders for **side outer borders**. If measurements are not the same, make some of the seams in borders slightly larger or smaller as needed. Matching centers and corners, sew side outer borders to quilt top.

6. Sew 1 **Border Triangle-Square** to each end of remaining outer borders to make 2 **top/bottom outer borders**. Measure *width* across center of quilt top (including added borders). Measure length of top/bottom outer borders. If measurements are not the same, make some of the seams in borders slightly larger or smaller as needed. Matching centers and corners, sew top/bottom outer borders to quilt top.

Completing the Quilt

1. To help stabilize the edges and prevent any seams from separating, stay-stitch around the quilt top approximately ¹/₈" from the edge.

2. Follow **Quilting**, page 108, to mark, layer, and quilt as desired. Quilt shown was machine quilted. Blocks were quilted with a combination of straight lines, curved lines, and swirls. The borders were quilted with feather patterns.

3. Follow **Making a Hanging Sleeve**, page 109, if a hanging sleeve is desired.

4. Cut a 28" square of binding fabric. Follow **Binding**, page 110, to bind quilt using 2"w bias binding with mitered corners.

Strip Set
(make 6)

Unit 6
(make 24)

4¹/₂"

Fig. 3

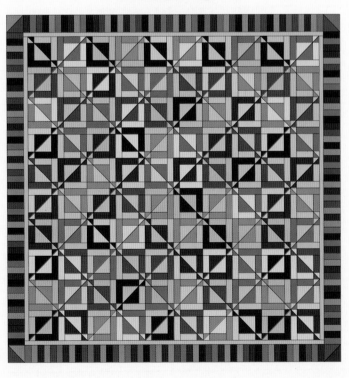

Border Triangle-Square (make 4)

Quilt Top Diagram

Elizabeth

Quilted by Amber Coffey.

Finished Quilt Size:
68¹/₂" x 68¹/₂"
(174 cm x 174 cm)

Finished Block Size:
8" x 8" (20 cm x 20 cm)

Like several of Carrie's quilts, Elizabeth began with a particular fabric collection—in this instance, a fabric line that Carrie loved at first sight. It was important to Carrie that she balance the placement of darker fabrics without making the quilt look too planned. She decided to use blocks made in such a way that they suggested they had been made at different times and for different projects. It took a while for Carrie to name this quilt. "In trying to think of something that sounded old and old-fashioned, I started considering [women's] names. As it turns out, my Mom's mother was named Elizabeth. Perfect!"

Yardage Requirements

Yardage is based on 43"/44" (109 cm/112 cm) wide fabric. Fat quarters are approximately 21" x 18" (53 cm x 46 cm).

$1^1/_8$ yds (1 m) of tan print #1 fabric for Star Blocks

$^3/_4$ yd (69 cm) of tan print #2 fabric for Delectable Mountain Blocks

6 fat quarters of assorted tan print #3 fabrics

8 fat quarters of assorted pink print fabrics

3 fat quarters of assorted brown print fabrics

2 fat quarters of assorted blue print fabrics

4 fat quarters of assorted burgundy print fabrics

$^7/_8$ yd (80 cm) of fabric for binding

$4^3/_8$ yds (4 m) of fabric for backing

You will also need:

77" x 77" (196 cm x 196 cm) piece of batting

Cutting Out the Pieces

*Follow **Rotary Cutting**, page 105, to cut fabric. All measurements include $^1/_4$" seam allowances.*

From tan print #1 fabric:

- Cut 4 strips $5^1/_4$" wide by the width of fabric. From these strips,
  - Cut 24 **large squares** $5^1/_4$" x $5^1/_4$".
- Cut 6 strips $2^1/_2$" wide by the width of fabric. From these strips,
  - Cut 96 **very small squares** $2^1/_2$" x $2^1/_2$".

From tan print #2 fabric:

- Cut 6 strips $2^7/_8$" wide by the width of fabric. From these strips,
  - Cut 72 **small squares** $2^7/_8$" x $2^7/_8$".
- Cut 2 strips $2^1/_2$" wide by the width of fabric. From these strips,
  - Cut 24 **very small squares** $2^1/_2$" x $2^1/_2$".

From *each* tan print #3 fat quarter:

- Cut 1 strip $6^7/_8$" x 21". From this strip,
  - Cut 2 **very large squares** $6^7/_8$" x $6^7/_8$". Cut a total of 12 very large squares.
- Cut 2 strips $4^1/_2$" x 21". From these strips,
  - Cut 8 **medium squares** $4^1/_2$" x $4^1/_2$". Cut a total of 48 medium squares.

From *each* pink print fat quarters:

- Cut 1 strip 7" x 21". From this strip,
  - Cut 2 squares 7" x 7". Cut a total of 12 squares. Cut each square *twice* diagonally to make a total of 48 **triangles**.
  - Cut 1 **very large square** $6^7/_8$" x $6^7/_8$". Cut a total of 8 very large squares.
- Cut 1 strip $6^7/_8$" x 21". From this strip,
  - Cut 1 **very large square** $6^7/_8$" x $6^7/_8$". Cut a total of 4 very large squares. You will have 12 very large squares.

From remainder of strip,

  - Cut 1 strip $4^1/_2$" x $14^1/_8$". From this strip,
    - Cut 3 **medium squares** $4^1/_2$" x $4^1/_2$". Cut a total of 24 medium squares.

From *each* brown print fat quarter:

- Cut 4 strips $2^7/_8$" x 21". From these strips,
  - Cut 24 **small squares** $2^7/_8$" x $2^7/_8$". Cut a total of 72 small squares (24 sets of 3 matching squares).

From *each* blue print fat quarter:

- Cut 3 strips $4^1/_2$" x 21". From these strips,
  - Cut 12 **medium squares** $4^1/_2$" x $4^1/_2$". Cut a total of 24 medium squares.

From *each* burgundy print fat quarter:

- Cut 4 strips $2^7/_8$" x 21". From these strips,
  - Cut 24 **small squares** $2^7/_8$" x $2^7/_8$". Cut a total of 96 (24 sets of 4 matching) small squares.

Making the Triangle-Squares

Follow **Piecing**, page 106, and **Pressing**, page 107, to assemble the quilt top. Because there are so many seams in this quilt, you may need to use a seam allowance slightly smaller than the usual $^1/_4$". As you sew, measure your work to compare with the measurements provided and adjust your seam allowance as needed.

1. Draw a diagonal line (corner to corner) on wrong side of each tan print #2 **small square** and each tan print #3 **very large square**.

2. Matching right sides, place 1 tan print #2 **small square** on top of 1 brown **small square**. Stitch $^1/_4$" from each side of drawn line (Fig. 1). Cut along drawn line and press seam allowances to brown fabric to make 2 Small Triangle-Squares. Small Triangle-Square should measure $2^1/_2$" x $2^1/_2$" including seam allowances. Make a total of 144 Small Triangle-Squares.

Fig. 1

Small Triangle-Square
(make 144)

3. Use tan print #3 **very large squares** and pink **very large squares** to make 24 Large Triangle-Squares. Press seam allowances to pink fabric. Large Triangle-Square should measure $6^1/2$" x $6^1/2$" including seam allowances.

Making the Flying Geese

1. Draw a diagonal line (corner to corner) on wrong side of each burgundy print **small square**.
2. For 4 matching **Flying Geese**, select 4 matching burgundy **small squares** and 1 tan print #1 **large square**.
3. Matching right sides, place 1 **small square** on opposite corners of **large square** (Fig. 2); pin in place.
4. Stitch $1/4$" from each side of drawn lines (Fig. 3). Cut along drawn lines to make 2 Unit 1's. Press seam allowances to burgundy fabric.
5. Matching corners, place 1 **small square** on each **Unit 1** (Fig. 4).
6. Stitch seam $1/4$" from each side of drawn lines (Fig. 5). Cut along drawn lines to make 4 Flying Geese. Press seam allowances to burgundy fabric. Flying Geese should measure $2^1/2$" x $4^1/2$" including seam allowances.
7. Repeat Steps 2–6 to make 24 sets of 4 matching Flying Geese.

Making the Delectable Mountain Blocks

Press seam allowances open or as indicated by arrows in diagrams.

1. For each **Delectable Mountain Block**, select 6 matching **Small Triangle Squares**, 1 tan print #2 **very small square**, and 1 **Large Triangle-Square**.
2. Sew 3 **Small Triangle-Squares** together to make Unit 2.
3. Sew 3 **Small Triangle-Squares** and **very small square** together to make Unit 3.

Large Triangle-Square (make 24)

Fig. 2

Fig. 3

Unit 1 (make 2)

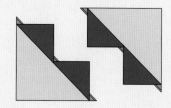

Fig. 4

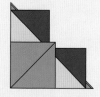

Fig. 5

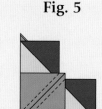

Flying Geese (make 24 sets of 4 matching)

Unit 2

Unit 3

4. Sew **Large Triangle-Square** and **Unit 2** together to make **Unit 4**.
5. Sew **Unit 3** and **Unit 4** together to make **Delectable Mountain Block**. Delectable Mountain Block should measure $8^{1}/_{2}$" x $8^{1}/_{2}$" including seam allowances.
6. Repeat Steps 1–5 to make 24 Delectable Mountain Blocks.

Making the Star Blocks

1. For each **Star Block**, select 4 matching **Flying Geese**, 4 tan print #1 **very small squares**, and 1 blue print **medium square**.
2. Sew 2 tan print #1 **very small squares** and 1 **Flying Geese** together to make **Unit 5**. Press seam allowances to very small squares. Make 2 Unit 5's.
3. Sew 2 **Flying Geese** and 1 **medium square** together to make **Unit 6**. Press seam allowances to medium square.
4. Sew 2 **Unit 5's** and **Unit 6** together to make **Star Block**. Press seam allowances to Unit 6. Star Block should measure $8^{1}/_{2}$" x $8^{1}/_{2}$" including seam allowances.
5. Repeat Steps 1–4 to make 24 Star Blocks.

Making the Four Patch Blocks

1. Sew 1 pink **medium square** and 1 tan print #3 **medium square** together to make **Unit 7**. Press seam allowances open or to one side. Make 2 Unit 7's.
2. Sew 2 **Unit 7's** together to make **Four Patch Block**. To press seam allowances, follow **Collapsing the Seams**, page 107. Four Patch Block should measure $8^{1}/_{2}$" x $8^{1}/_{2}$" including seam allowances.
3. Repeat Steps 1–2 to make 12 Four Patch Blocks.

Making the Setting Triangles

1. Sew 1 tan print #3 **medium square** and 2 pink **triangles** together to make **side setting triangle**. Press seam allowances open or to triangles. Make 24 side setting triangles.
2. Sew 2 **side setting triangles** together to make **corner setting triangle**. Press seam allowances open or to one side. Make 4 corner setting triangles.

Unit 4

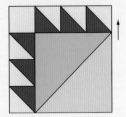

Delectable Mountain Block (make 24)

Unit 5 (make 2)

Unit 6

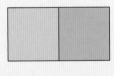

Star Block (make 24)

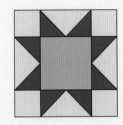

Unit 7 (make 2)

Four Patch Block (make 12)

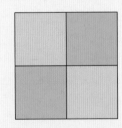

Side Setting Triangle (make 24)

Corner Setting Triangles (make 4)

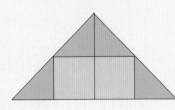

Assembling the Quilt Top

*Referring to **Assembly Diagram**, arrange **Blocks**, **side setting triangles**, and **corner setting triangles** into diagonal **Rows**.*

1. Sew **Blocks** and **side setting triangles** together into **Rows**. Press seam allowances open or press them in one direction in every other Row and in the opposite direction in remaining Rows.

2. Sew **Rows** together, pressing seam allowances open or in one direction.

3. Sew **corner setting triangles** to quilt top. Press seam allowances open or to corner setting triangles. Quilt top should measure approximately $68^1/_2$" x $68^1/_2$" including seam allowances.

Completing the Quilt

1. To help stabilize the edges and prevent any seams from separating, stay-stitch around the quilt top approximately $^1/_8$" from the edge.

2. Follow **Quilting**, page 108, to mark, layer, and quilt as desired. Quilt shown was machine quilted with variegated thread in an all-over floral pattern.

3. Follow **Making a Hanging Sleeve**, page 109, if a hanging sleeve is desired.

4. Cut a 26" square of binding fabric. Follow **Binding**, page 110, to bind quilt using 2"w bias binding with mitered corners.

Note: To make your quilt larger, you might add one or more plain fabric borders.

To add additional Blocks, you might begin with 4 Four Patch Blocks in the center. Add "rounds" to the center in this order: Delectable Mountain Blocks, Star Blocks, Four Patch Blocks, Star Blocks, Delectable Mountain Blocks, and setting triangles. This would require 20 Four Patch Blocks, 32 Delectable Mountain Blocks, 32 Star Blocks, 20 setting triangles, and 4 corner setting triangles.

Assembly Diagram

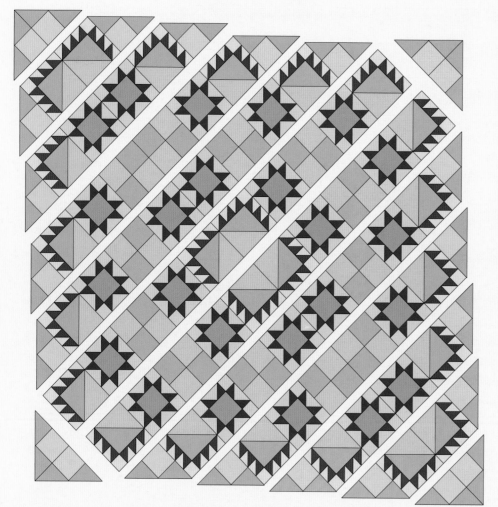

General Instructions

To make your quilting easier and more enjoyable, we encourage you to carefully read all of the general instructions, study the color photographs, and familiarize yourself with the individual project instructions before beginning a project.

Fabrics

Selecting Fabrics

Choose high-quality, medium-weight 100% cotton fabrics. All-cotton fabrics hold a crease better, fray less, and are easier to quilt than cotton/polyester blends.

Yardage requirements listed for each project are based on 43"/44" wide fabric with a "usable" width of 40" after shrinkage and trimming selvages. Actual usable width will probably vary slightly from fabric to fabric. Our recommended yardage lengths should be adequate for occasional re-squaring of fabric when many cuts are required.

While the size of fat quarters may vary slightly, each should be at least 21" x 18" (53 x 46 cm). If they are smaller, more fat quarters may be required.

Preparing Fabrics

We do not recommend pre-washing your fabric. Pre-washing fabrics may cause edges to ravel. As a result, your fat quarters may not be large enough to cut all of the pieces required for your chosen project. Therefore, we do not recommend pre-washing your yardage or fat quarters. Refer to **Caring for Your Quilt**, page 112, for instructions on washing your finished quilt.

Before cutting, prepare fabrics with a steam iron set on cotton and starch or sizing (such as Best Press™ Sizing/Clear Starch Alternative). The starch or sizing will give the fabric a crisp finish. This will make cutting more accurate and may make piecing easier.

Rotary Cutting

Rotary cutting has brought speed and accuracy to quiltmaking by allowing quilters to easily cut strips of fabric and then cut those strips into smaller pieces. It is helpful to keep pieces separated and identified in zip top bags.

Cutting from Fat Quarters
- Place fabric flat on work surface with lengthwise (18") edge closest to you.
- Cut all strips parallel to 21" edge of the fabric unless otherwise indicated in project instructions.
- To cut each strip required for a project, place ruler over left edge of fabric, aligning desired marking on ruler with left edge; make cut.

Cutting from Yardages
- Place fabric yardage on work surface with fold closest to you.
- Cut all strips from the selvage-to-selvage width of the fabric unless otherwise indicated in project instructions.

- Square left edge of fabric using rotary cutter and rulers (Figs. 1 – 2).
- To cut each strip required for a project, place ruler over cut edge of fabric, aligning desired marking on ruler with cut edge; make cut (Fig. 3).
- When cutting several strips from a single piece of fabric, it is important to make sure that cuts remain at a perfect right angle to the fold; square fabric as needed.

Piecing

Precise cutting, followed by accurate piecing, will ensure that all pieces of quilt top fit together well.

- Set sewing machine stitch length for approximately 11 stitches per inch.
- Use neutral-colored general-purpose sewing thread (not quilting thread) in needle and in bobbin.
- A consistent seam allowance is *essential*. Because there are so many seams in each of the quilts in this book, you may need to use a seam allowance slightly smaller than the usual $1/4$". As you sew, measure your work to compare with the measurements provided in the project instructions and adjust your seam allowance as needed. Presser feet that are $1/4$" wide are available for most sewing machines.
- When piecing, always place pieces right sides together and match raw edges; pin if necessary.
- Chain piecing saves time and will usually result in more accurate piecing.
- Trim away points of seam allowances that extend beyond edges of sewn pieces.

Sewing Strip Sets

When there are several strips to assemble into a strip set, first sew strips together into pairs, then sew pairs together to form strip set. To help avoid distortion, sew seams in opposite directions (Fig. 4).

Sewing Across Seam Intersections

When sewing across intersection of two seams, place pieces right sides together and match seams exactly, making sure seam allowances are pressed in opposite directions (Fig. 5).

Fig. 1

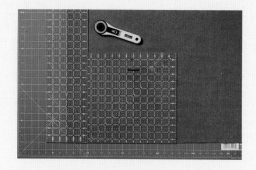

Fig. 2

Fig. 3

Fig. 4

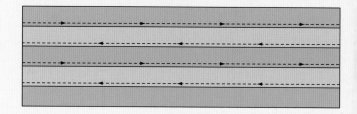

Fig. 5

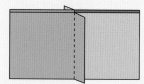

Sewing Sharp Points

To ensure sharp points when joining triangular or diagonal pieces, stitch across the center of the "X" (shown in pink) formed on wrong side by previous seams (Fig. 6).

Pressing

For years, hand quilters have pressed seam allowances to one side to prevent seams from pulling open. Since most of us now use sewing machines, the stitches are smaller and tighter. Also, the fabrics, thread, and batting we use today are better quality. Consequently, we have fewer concerns about any weaknesses that might arise when seam allowances are pressed open. Pressing seam allowances open may make points sharper and will result in less bulk when adjacent points are joined. However, pressing the seams open may make quilting in the ditch more difficult. In the end, it is entirely a personal choice.

- Use steam iron set on "Cotton" for all pressing.
- Press after sewing each seam.
- Suggestions for pressing seam allowances are provided with each project.
- To prevent dark fabric seam allowance from showing through light fabric, trim darker seam allowance slightly narrower than lighter seam allowance.
- To press long seams, such as those in long strip sets, without curving or other distortion, lay strips across width of the ironing board.

Collapsing the Seams

When pressing where 2 seams intersect, such as the center of a Four Patch, "collapsing the seams" will reduce bulk. To "collapse the seam," use a seam ripper to remove the stitches that are in the seam allowances of the seam just made (Fig. 7). Press seam allowances clockwise. At the seam intersection, press the seam allowances open so that the center lies flat (Fig. 8).

Invisible Appliqué

1. Pin stabilizer, such as paper or any of the commercially available products, on wrong side of background fabric before stitching appliqués in place.
2. Thread sewing machine with clear or smoke monofilament thread; use general-purpose thread that matches background fabric in bobbin.
3. Set sewing machine for a medium (approximately 1/8") zigzag stitch and a short stitch length. Slightly loosening the top tension may yield a smoother stitch.
4. Begin by stitching two or three stitches in place (drop feed dogs or set stitch length at 0) to anchor thread. Most of the zigzag stitch should be on the appliqué with the right edge of the stitch falling at the outside edge of the appliqué. Stitch over all exposed raw edges of appliqué pieces.
5. When stitching outside curves (Fig. 9), stop with needle in background fabric. Raise presser foot and pivot project as needed with needle in fabric (indicated by dots). Lower presser foot and continue stitching, pivoting as often as necessary to follow curve.
6. Do not backstitch at end of stitching. Pull threads to wrong side of background fabric; knot thread and trim ends.
7. Carefully tear away stabilizer.

Fig. 6

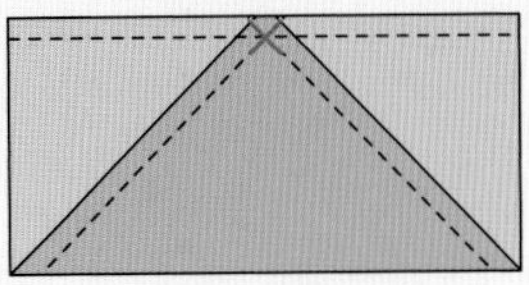

Fig. 7

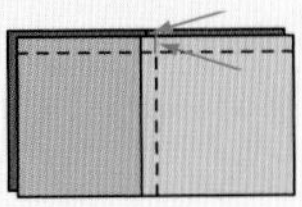

Fig. 8

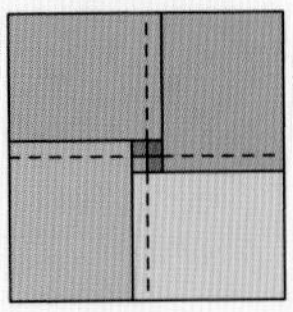

Fig. 9

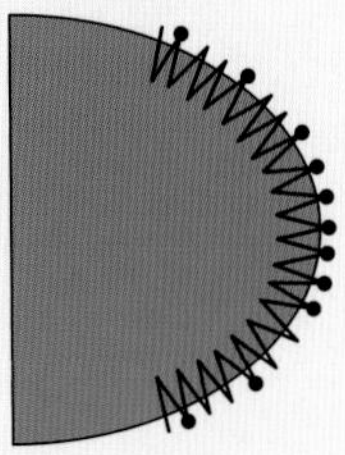

*Quilting holds the three layers (top, batting, and backing) of the quilt together and can be done by hand or machine. Because marking, layering, and quilting are interrelated and may be done in different orders depending on circumstances, please read entire **Quilting** section, pages 108 – 109, before beginning project.*

Marking Quilting Lines

Quilting lines may be marked using fabric marking pencils, chalk markers, or water- or air-soluble pens.

Simple quilting designs may be marked with chalk or chalk pencil after basting. A small area may be marked, then quilted, before moving to next area to be marked. Intricate designs should be marked before basting using a more durable marker.

Caution: Pressing may permanently set some marks. **Test** different markers **on scrap fabric** to find one that marks clearly and can be thoroughly removed.

A wide variety of pre-cut quilting stencils, as well as entire books of quilting patterns, are available. Using a stencil makes it easier to mark intricate or repetitive designs.

To make a stencil from a pattern, center template plastic over pattern and use a permanent marker to trace pattern onto plastic. Use a craft knife with single or double blade to cut channels along traced lines (Fig. 10).

Fig. 10

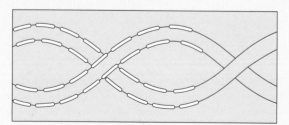

Preparing the Backing

To allow for slight shifting of quilt top during quilting, backing should be approximately 4" larger on all sides. Yardage requirements listed for quilt backings are calculated for 43"/44"w fabric. Using 90"w or 108"w fabric for the backing of a bed-sized quilt may eliminate piecing. To piece a backing using 43"/44"w fabric, use the following instructions.

1. Measure length and width of quilt top; add 8" to each measurement.

2. **If determined width is 79" or less,** cut backing fabric into two lengths slightly longer than determined *length* measurement. Trim selvages. Place lengths with right sides facing and sew long edges together, forming tube (Fig. 11). Match seams and press along one fold (Fig. 12). Cut along pressed fold to form single piece (Fig. 13).

3. **If determined width is more than 79",** it may require less fabric yardage if the backing is pieced horizontally. Divide determined *length* measurement by 40" to determine how many widths will be needed. Cut required number of widths the determined *width* measurement. Trim selvages. Sew long edges together to form single piece.

4. Trim backing to size determined in Step 1; press seam allowances open.

Fig. 11	Fig. 12	Fig. 13

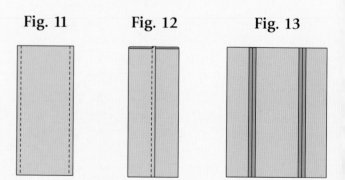

Choosing the Batting

The appropriate batting will make quilting easier. For fine hand quilting, choose low-loft batting. All cotton or cotton/polyester blend battings work well for machine quilting because the cotton helps "grip" quilt layers. If quilt is to be tied, a high-loft batting, sometimes called extra-loft or fat batting, may be used to make quilt "fluffy."

Types of batting include cotton, polyester, wool, cotton/polyester blend, cotton/wool blend, and silk.

When selecting batting, refer to package labels for characteristics and care instructions. Cut batting same size as prepared backing.

Assembling the Quilt

1. Examine wrong side of quilt top closely; trim any seam allowances and clip any threads that may show through front of the quilt. Press quilt top, being careful not to "set" any marked quilting lines.

2. Place backing *wrong* side up on flat surface. Use masking tape to tape edges of backing to surface. Place batting on top of backing fabric. Smooth batting gently, being careful not to stretch or tear. Center quilt top *right* side up on batting.

3. Use 1" rustproof safety pins to "pin-baste" all layers together, spacing pins approximately 4" apart. Begin at center and work toward outer edges to secure all layers. If possible, place pins away from areas that will be quilted, although pins may be removed as needed when quilting.

Quilting Methods

Use general-purpose thread in bobbin. Do not use quilting thread. Thread the needle of machine with general-purpose thread or transparent monofilament thread to make quilting blend with quilt top fabrics. Use decorative thread, such as a metallic or contrasting-color general-purpose thread, to make quilting lines stand out more.

Straight-Line Quilting

The term "straight-line" is somewhat deceptive, since curves (especially gentle ones) as well as straight lines can be stitched with this technique.

1. Set stitch length for six to ten stitches per inch and attach walking foot to sewing machine.

2. Determine which section of quilt will have longest continuous quilting line, oftentimes area from center top to center bottom. Roll up and secure each edge of quilt to help reduce the bulk, keeping fabrics smooth.

3. Begin stitching on longest quilting line, using very short stitches for the first $1/4$" to "lock" quilting. Stitch across project, using one hand on each side of walking foot to slightly spread fabric and to guide fabric through machine. Lock stitches at end of quilting line.

4. Continue machine quilting, stitching longer quilting lines first to stabilize quilt before moving on to other areas.

Free-Motion Quilting

Free-motion quilting may be free form or may follow a marked pattern.

1. Attach darning foot to sewing machine and lower or cover feed dogs.

2. Position quilt under darning foot; lower foot. Holding top thread, take a stitch and pull bobbin thread to top of quilt. To "lock" beginning of quilting line, hold top and bobbin threads while making three to five stitches in place.

3. Use one hand on each side of darning foot to slightly spread fabric and to move fabric through the machine. Even stitch length is achieved by using smooth, flowing hand motion and steady machine speed. Slow machine speed and fast hand movement will create long stitches. Fast machine speed and slow hand movement will create short stitches. Move quilt sideways, back and forth, in a circular motion, or in a random motion to create desired designs; do not rotate quilt. Lock stitches at end of each quilting line.

Making a Hanging Sleeve

Attaching a hanging sleeve to back of wall hanging or quilt before the binding is added allows project to be displayed on a wall.

1. Measure width of quilt top edge and subtract 1". Cut piece of fabric 7"w by determined measurement.

2. Press short edges of fabric piece $1/4$" to wrong side; press edges $1/4$" to wrong side again and machine stitch in place.

3. Matching wrong sides, fold piece in half lengthwise to form tube.

4. Follow project instructions to sew binding to quilt top and to trim backing and batting. Before Blindstitching binding to backing, match raw edges and stitch hanging sleeve to center top edge on back of quilt.

5. Finish binding quilt, treating hanging sleeve as part of backing.

6. Blindstitch bottom of hanging sleeve to backing, taking care not to stitch through to front of quilt.

7. Insert dowel or slat into hanging sleeve.

Binding

Making Continuous Bias Strip Binding

Bias strips for binding can simply be cut and pieced to desired length. However, when a long length of binding is needed, the "continuous" method is quick and accurate.

1. Cut square from binding fabric the size indicated in project instructions. Cut square in half diagonally to make two triangles.

2. With right sides together and using $1/4$" seam allowance, sew triangles together (Fig. 14); press seam allowances open.

3. On wrong side of fabric, draw lines the width of binding as specified in project instructions, usually 2"(Fig. 15). Cut off any remaining fabric less than this width.

4. With right sides inside, bring short edges together to form tube; match raw edges so that first drawn line of top section meets second drawn line of bottom section (Fig. 16).

5. Carefully pin edges together by inserting pins through drawn lines at point where drawn lines intersect, making sure pins go through intersections on both sides. Using $1/4$" seam allowance, sew edges together; press seam allowances open.

6. To cut continuous strip, begin cutting along first drawn line (Fig. 17). Continue cutting along drawn line around tube.

7. Trim ends of bias strip square.

8. Matching wrong sides and raw edges, carefully press bias strip in half lengthwise to complete binding.

Fig. 14

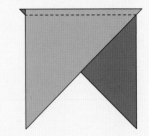

Fig. 15

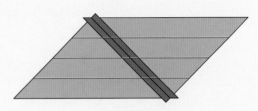

Fig. 16

Fig. 17

Attaching Binding with Mitered Corners

1. Beginning with one end near center on bottom edge of quilt, lay binding around quilt to make sure that seams in binding will not end up at a corner. Adjust placement if necessary. Matching raw edges of binding to raw edge of quilt top, pin binding to right side of quilt along one edge.

2. When you reach first corner, mark $1/4$" from corner of quilt top (Fig. 18).

3. Beginning approximately 10" from end of binding and using $1/4$" seam allowance, sew binding to quilt, backstitching at beginning of stitching and at mark (Fig. 19). Lift needle out of fabric and clip thread.

4. Fold binding as shown in Figs. 20 – 21 and pin binding to adjacent side, matching raw edges. When you've reached the next corner, mark $1/4$" from edge of quilt top.

5. Backstitching at edge of quilt top, sew pinned binding to quilt (Fig. 22); backstitch at the next mark. Lift needle out of fabric and clip thread.

6. Continue sewing binding to quilt, stopping approximately 10" from starting point (Fig. 23).

7. Bring beginning and end of binding to center of opening and fold each end back, leaving a $1/4$" space between folds (Fig. 24). Finger press folds.

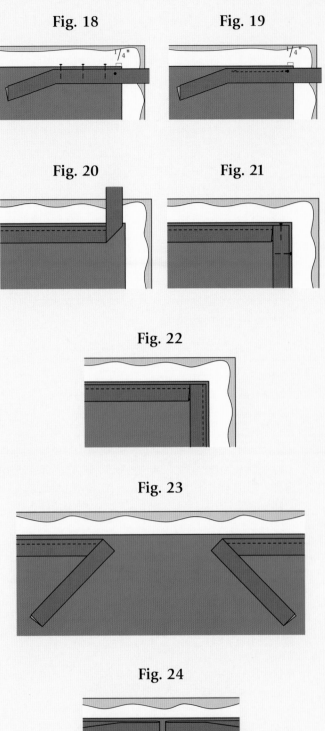

Fig. 18

Fig. 19

Fig. 20

Fig. 21

Fig. 22

Fig. 23

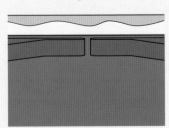

Fig. 24

8. Unfold ends of binding and draw a line across wrong side in finger-pressed crease. Draw a line through the lengthwise pressed fold of binding at the same spot to create a cross mark. With edge of ruler at cross mark, line up 45° angle marking on ruler with one long side of binding. Draw a diagonal line from edge to edge. Repeat on remaining end, making sure that the two diagonal lines are angled the same way (Fig. 25).

9. Matching right sides and diagonal lines, pin binding ends together at right angles (Fig. 26).

10. Machine stitch along diagonal line (Fig. 27), removing pins as you stitch.

11. Lay binding against quilt to double check that it is correct length.

12. Trim binding ends, leaving 1/4" seam allowance; press seam open. Stitch binding to quilt.

13. Trim backing and batting even with edges of quilt top.

14. On one edge of quilt, fold binding over to quilt backing and pin pressed edge in place, covering stitching line (Fig. 28). On adjacent side, fold binding over, forming a mitered corner (Fig. 29). Repeat to pin remainder of binding in place.

15. Blindstitch binding to backing, taking care not to stitch through to front of quilt. To Blindstitch, come up at 1, go down at 2, and come up at 3 (Fig. 30). Length of stitches may be varied as desired.

Caring for Your Quilt

• Wash finished quilt in cold water on gentle cycle with mild soap. Soaps such as Orvus® Paste or Charlie's Soap®, which have no softeners, fragrances, whiteners, or other additives, are safest. Rinse twice in cold water.

• Use a dye magnet, such as Shout® Color Catcher®, each time quilt is washed to absorb any dyes that bleed. When washing quilt the first time, you may choose to use two color catchers for extra caution.

• Dry quilt on low heat/air fluff in 15 minute increments until dry.

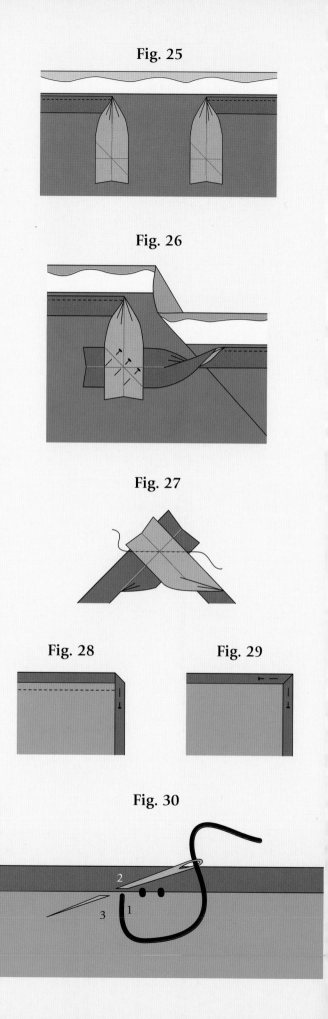

Fig. 25

Fig. 26

Fig. 27

Fig. 28   Fig. 29

Fig. 30